Endorsements

Bob and Evelyn McDonald have given us another marvelous gift with their new book, 'Windows on Nature: Reflections on God'. With exquisitely beautiful nature photographs of Australia and New Zealand alongside stories, prayers, and reflections drawn from science, Indigenous wisdom, and Scripture, they throw open windows on God's creation that provide stunning vistas onto life and faith. The joy of reading—no, experiencing—this book will be eclipsed only by the delight readers will have as they turn from its pages and step out themselves into a world seen afresh in all its wonder and complexity and discover, thanks to the McDonalds, more clearly who God is and who we are called to be.

Dr Jonathan Moo, Professor of New Testament and Environmental Studies, Whitworth University, Spokane, Washington. Author of a number of books including *Creation Care: A Biblical Theology of the Natural World*

When the psalmist looked upwards and saw a breathtaking sunset, or the cloud-strewn heavens, or a starry night sky, he saw it as the earth praising its creator. 'They pour forth speech', he enthused. 'They use no words; no sound is heard from them. Yet their voice goes out into all the earth, their words to the ends of the world.' Bob and Evelyn McDonald are just like that psalmist. They don't just see nature worshipping God, they capture those moments in their exquisite photographs. Together with their reflections and prayers, this collection had me singing along with the psalmist, 'The earth declares the glory of God.'

Dr Michael Frost, Author, Founding Director Tinsley Institute, Morling College, Sydney, Australia

How much we need the natural world to feed and replenish our spirits in these troubled times. This book does that in spades, with helpful reflections centering our thoughts on the Giver and Sustainer of life.

Rev Tim Costello AO, Author, Senior Fellow Australian Centre for Public Christianity, Executive Director Micah Australia

Through a feast of remarkable photographs, and eyes and ears for the nuances of Scripture and the colours of Australia, Bob and Evelyn give us unique perspectives on God's gifts to us of landscapes and creatures. Like Solomon (1 Kings 4:32-33) their joy and delight at God's creation wisdom beckons us to worship Christ, in whom and for whom all things were created and hold together.

Rev Anthony Brammall, Vice Principal, Sydney Missionary and Bible College, Australia

What a beautiful book that powerfully displays how God speaks not only through his word in the Bible but also in the splendour and intricacy of his creation! 'Windows on Nature: Reflections on God' provides a unique insight into the natural world of Australia and New Zealand, painting a vivid picture of a God who delights in all that he has made. May we be inspired to play our part in taking care of this amazing world.

Dr Ruth Valerio, Global Advocacy and Influencing Director, Tearfund UK

This book makes me homesick to go see it all. I weep at the abundance of beauty. I see God's spirit hovering over the waters, the mountains, the starry host. Inexpressable contrast of colours sensing the Glory beyond. Creation shouts to invite us to be connected with God as he upholds everything by the power of his word. Our response is to bow in humble adoration and proclaim: 'My God, how GREAT Thou art'.

Aunty Donna Meehan from Gamilaroi Nation, International Author and Broadcaster

This book is pure joy. The pictures celebrate the colours, the beauty and the richness of creation. The background information is well researched and stimulates the mind. Most of all, this explosion of beauty and abundance leads naturally to reflections on the Creator, worship and prayer. Many thanks to Evelyn and Bob for this precious gift.

Professor Thomas Nann, Sustainable Energy Researcher, Head of School of Information and Physical Sciences, University of Newcastle, Australia

Through the eyes of faith, one can see the Creator through the creation. Bob and Evelyn McDonald's new book continues where 'A Nature Lover's Guide to Seeing God' left off. Exquisite photographs of these beautiful lands now called Australia, together with scientifically informed background material, thoughtful reflections and succinct prayers will sharpen your sight.

Dr Mick Pope, Ecotheologian and Author, Australia

'Windows on Nature: Reflections on God' is a superb book drawing our attention to the incredible beauty and wonder of God's creation. Stunning photography combined with consistently Biblical reflections generate a longing to know more of the One who made us and all things well. Every chapter leads the reader gently from God's general revelation in creation to God's special revelation in his word. I know that this book will encourage and edify all who read it as God's glory is amplified from start to finish. And so, I thoroughly commend it to you.

Right Revd Rod Chiswell, Bishop, Anglican Diocese of Armidale, Australia

Authors Bob and Evelyn McDonald echo the Psalmist's claim 'the earth is the LORD'S and everything in it' (Psalm 24:1) through the pages of this book. Each reflection supplements beautiful photography with intellectual rigour, theological clarity and emotional warmth. The invitation to see God within creation is also an invitation for us to see ourselves (and each other) more clearly: created and creative. A wonderful devotional study.

Rev Andrew Palmer, Manager, Missional Communities, Wesley Mission Australia

I am appreciating the opportunity to be still and meditate on 'Windows on Nature: Reflections on God' for the visual pleasure of exquisite photography amplified by well-researched science, all pointing to the glory of the Creator. Authors Bob and Evelyn communicate the importance of watching, listening and reflecting as spiritual disciplines. If you can tear yourself away from the magnificent cover photo, turn to Reflection 10 on the donkey orchid and be amazed by the complexity of its lifecycle. Without any power of its own, this delicate plant beautifying our bushland is a lesson in humility-as-strength. In a world that worships power in many forms, this unpretentious orchid is a reminder of the enduring values to live by that we find in the life of Mary and her son Jesus, Saviour of the World.

Rev Dr Phillip Marshall, Missiologist, SIM International

Bob and Evelyn have a unique way of opening up our eyes to the magnificence and grandeur of God as they explore, with such profound attention to detail, the intricacies of creation. As you read this you will find that it speaks deeply to your soul. You will grow to understand more fully how the God who created everything with such love and attention to the finest detail of every plant and animal, cares so greatly about every aspect of your life and for you, whom he also created with loving detail.

Pastor Sue Irwin, Senior Pastor, The Grainery Church, Newcastle, Australia

God has gifted us the most magnificent common home here on earth where life flourishes. And despite our significant scientific endeavours, we have not yet found a planet anywhere where we can survive, let alone thrive, like we do here on earth. 'Windows on Nature: Reflections on God' is a sublimely beautiful collection of scripture, images and reflections that remind us of just how spectacular the gift of God's creation is, both here on earth and out into the stars.

Jane Kelly, Creation and Climate Justice Coordinator, Common Grace, Australia

Blue Gum Publishing
Website: www.bluegumpublishing.com
Email: enquiries@bluegumpublishing.com
Newcastle, NSW, Australia

Cataloguing in Publication Data:
Title: Windows on Nature: Reflections on God
ISBN: 978-0-6450446-6-9
Subjects: Nature; Creation; Christianity; Photography; Science

Natural history illustrations (pages 45-49): Lillian Webb Graphic
Copy edit: Capstone Editing

Front cover photograph: Aerial photograph at James Price Point, Kimberley, Western Australia.
Rear cover photograph: Sunset over the ocean from Lady Elliott Island, Queensland.
Acknowledgements photograph: Aerial view of Tjoritja / West MacDonnell Ranges, Northern Territory
Foreword photograph: Aerial view of tidal mangroves, Broome, Western Australia.
Introduction photograph: Waterfall flowing into Regan's Pool, Hancock Gorge, Karijini National Park, Western Australia.
Most land-based photographs were taken with a Fujifilm X-T1, X-T2 or X-T4 camera using a range of Fujinon XF lenses. The underwater photos in Reflections 20 and 27 were taken with a GoPro Hero 9 Black camera (with a six-inch dome) and an Olympus TG-5 camera, respectively. Aerial (drone) photographs were taken with a DJI Mavic 2 Pro.

Windows on Nature: Reflections on God

BOB & EVELYN MCDONALD

Variegated fairy-wren (Malurus lamberti)

Acknowledgements

We would like to acknowledge the Traditional Custodians of the lands we have walked through, photographed and enjoyed, and recognise their continuing connection to land, waters and community. We pay our respects to them and Aboriginal and Torres Strait Islander Elders past, present and emerging. We are extremely grateful for the way they have cared for their lands for over 60,000 years, such that today we enjoy a country with incredible natural and cultural diversity and beauty.

We would also like to acknowledge the work that has been done over a number of generations in setting aside and managing, often with limited resources, our system of national parks, conservation areas and other areas of special natural and cultural significance.

We are very appreciative of those who have taken the time to read a draft copy of this book and provide the endorsements on pages 2 to 3. We are deeply grateful to Laureate Professor John Attia for writing the Foreword and providing very helpful feedback and encouragement. We would also like to thank Bev Murrill for her feedback on a draft copy and Rob Kyte who provided valuable support on the use of Adobe InDesign.

We are also grateful for those who purchased and read our first book, *A Nature Lover's Guide to Seeing God: Reflections and Photographs by a Biologist and a Pilgrim*. This, together with feedback that was provided, was a great encouragement to us in creating this second book.

We would also like to acknowledge the use of two photographs (Reflections 4 and 30) that were taken by our ecologist son, Dr Peter McDonald. All other photos were taken by us as we had the delightful privilege of exploring the beautiful natural world in Australia and New Zealand.

Contents

Foreword

In this second book, Bob and Evelyn continue to share their love of God's creation with readers, combining their stunning photographs with scientific information and spiritual insight. The effect of this winning combination is something that we too infrequently experience in our technological society: a sense of amazement and wonder.

This is something that is well described by King David in the Old Testament Psalms:

Let the heavens rejoice, let the earth be glad; let the sea resound, and all that is in it. Let the fields be jubilant, and everything in them; let all the trees of the forest sing for joy. (Psalm 96:11-12)

That sense of joy and wonder permeates every reflection in the book, sometimes tinged with puzzlement (the giant pink slugs of Reflection 5) and sometimes tinged with urgency and warning (the loss of our natural world in Reflection 32). Throughout the book, the effect is the same: to open our eyes to something amazing and wonderful, and to help us see in creation, the hand and the nature of a loving and creative God. Like the art critic who helps us recognise the hallmarks of a great artist in a famous canvas, Bob and Evelyn help us recognise the character of the artist behind our created world.

This physical world, which we tend to take for granted and even disrespect, as if it had no sacred association for us, abounds with the creative work of God. It resounds with his goodness and glory!

My prayer as you read this book is that your eyes will be opened to God's glory in new ways and that like the creatures in heaven, you, too, will be drawn to worship God and the Lamb, through whom all things were made and are sustained:

Then I heard every creature in heaven and on earth and under the earth and on the sea, and all that is in them, saying:
'To him who sits on the throne and to the Lamb
be praise and honor and glory and power,
for ever and ever!' (Revelation 5:13)

Venite adoremus. Come let us worship…

Laureate Professor John Attia
College of Health, Medicine and Wellbeing
University of Newcastle
Hunter Medical Research Institute (HMRI)

Introduction

Since we wrote our first book, *A Nature Lover's Guide to Seeing God*, the world has experienced a pandemic that has had dramatic effects on our lives. In response to the lockdowns that were brought in to limit the spread of the corona virus and keep people safe, there appears to have been a heightened appreciation of the simple freedom of being able to leave home and, in particular, enjoy the natural world. This may be a walk along a sandy beach, a swim in the clean salt water of the ocean, a stroll under the trees in a forest in the city or sitting on green grass in a park surrounded by flower beds pulsing with colour and the hum of bees. Research is increasingly showing that being in healthy natural environments has significant benefits—energising us, calming us, invigorating us and awakening connection-seeking in us.[1]

Spurred on by a heartfelt burden that we believe is from God to see the nature/creation, which benefits us so much and on which we all depend, cared for, and also encouraged by the positive response to our first book, we have undertaken to write this second one. In his spiritual classic, *Knowing God*, JI Packer writes that '*the modern spirit spawns great thoughts of man and leaves room only for small thoughts of God*'.[2] Through this book, it is our intention that the glory of God, who has brought into being and sustains creation, and his immense love for the world, so fully expressed in Jesus, are highlighted. May our response be great thoughts of God and greater love for him and the works of his hands and an outworking of this in our lives.

To this end, we are delighted to share with you more of our photographs to highlight something of the beauty, majesty, power, diversity, complexity, intricate detail and artistry in the natural world—God's wonderful creation through which he would speak to us all. Alongside these, we have included information gathered from scientific research as well as insights from Indigenous knowledge. We believe that the learnings from science, revealing how the various aspects of nature work, can draw us into even greater awe and appreciation of how wonderful the Creator of the universe is. Similarly, examples of the practices of the original custodians of the land we now call Australia indicate that they truly understood what it was to be caretakers of the land. Flowing from the images and background information are reflections based on texts from both the Old and New Testaments in the Bible. You might be surprised (as were we) by some of these. Each reflection is followed by a short prayer or meditation to make your own, or God may lead you in your own response to what you have read. In the middle of this book, we have included a new section, with its own introduction, containing five illustrated and mostly lesser-known but intriguing short stories from nature.

As we read, reflected and engaged in writing this book, we aimed to let God, through the scriptures, shape our views and not the other way round. This is not easy, as we all bring our own biases and cultural influences to our reading and interpretations of scripture. On the other hand, it is also easy to skip over or just not register verses or sections of text that appear not to be relevant or to match any preconceived ideas we may have. But we take seriously Paul's words to the church in Rome: '*Do not conform to the pattern of this world but be transformed by the renewing of your mind. Then you will be able to test and approve what God's will is—his good, pleasing and perfect will*' (Romans 12:2). In this, we believe what is so clearly expressed by John Stott: '*God intends our care of the creation to reflect our love for the Creator.*'[3] By this God is honoured and glorified.

Reflection 1:
Like a Tree

Background

In the photograph opposite, the canopy of a majestic 40-metre Sydney blue gum (*Eucalyptus saligna*) captures the early morning sunlight of a new day. The sunlight rapidly sets in motion the amazing process of photosynthesis. If we could look inside one of the green cells in the sunlit leaves, we would see its many chloroplasts starting to harvest light energy to produce sugars from carbon dioxide and water. The sugars will be distributed via the sugar pipelines (phloem) to growing regions of the tree or stored elsewhere. At the same time, the stomata —largely located on the underside of the leaves —are constantly monitoring environmental and hormonal signals to optimise photosynthesis and minimise water loss. Some of the older leaves are starting to drop off, and many more will be shed over summer. These will be replaced by new leaves with an average life span of 2 to 3 years.[4]

In the trunk, if we listen carefully with a stethoscope, we may hear crackling sounds from under the bark as water and dissolved minerals move upward through the hollow cells of the xylem.[5] On this warm day, around 200 kilograms of water will effortlessly flow from the roots to the top of the canopy against gravity, largely driven by sun-powered transpiration. The cells in the outer layer of bark are starting to dry out, before peeling off later in the season to be replaced by a beautiful new layer as the trunk expands.

Hidden from sight under the soil, the roots of the tree are in a symbiotic association with numerous fungal networks, mining the soil for nutrients, some of which have come from the recycling of shed leaves and bark.

Over an entire year, this tree will host a variety of animal life and will supply enough oxygen for four people and absorb an estimated 30 kilograms of carbon dioxide.[6,7,8]

Reflection

Trees! How I love being in a natural forest or seeing stands of trees along a riverbank. Some time ago on a day in late spring, we were assisting our son to erect a large, heavy sign in a desert park in Central Australia. From the cloudless sky, the sun blazed down, the heat almost palpable. The work was hot and very tiring. Nearby, a desert oak cast a broad, inviting shadow. We took a break to sit in the shade of this tree, enjoying the welcome respite it provided from the desert heat.

Most of us appreciate the benefits of trees without perhaps realising what incredible structures they are and how integral they are to God's created order on earth. Trees are referred to throughout the Bible, and one such example is in Psalm 1:

> *Blessed is the one who does not walk in step with the wicked or stand in the way that sinners take or sit in the company of mockers, but whose delight is in the law of the Lord, and who meditates on his law, day and night.* **That person is like a tree planted by streams of water, which yields its fruit in season and whose leaf does not wither— whatever they do prospers.** (Psalm 1:1-3)

The choices we make can have significant consequences in our own lives and in those of others. Psalm 1, in introducing the whole Book of Psalms, clearly sets out two ways of living— two choices. Choosing to be guided in life by the Creator of all life, God, is declared to result in a life that is likened to a flourishing tree.

According to the psalmist, this happens through reading God's law (the Torah)—in today's terms, the whole Bible. This reading leads us to '*delight in the law*'—to take genuine pleasure in God's word. Sometimes our reading of the Bible can feel laborious or legalistic—done as a chore or even as an unthinking habit—but even in such times, God can graciously imprint his words in our hearts and speak to us. On the other hand, when we stop and think that, through scripture, the God of the universe is revealing himself to us and that his word '*is alive and active*' (Hebrews 4:12), how can we not see what a privilege being able to read God's word is? It is a means by which we can increasingly know our Creator God, come to better understand ourselves and become increasingly familiar with his ways for us. Moreover, meditating regularly on his instruction, advice and teaching as our source of true life will shape who we are and how we live.

And, as the psalmist declares, as we delight in God's word and its active work in our lives, we become like a tree—a thriving tree. It is a beautiful picture! Is it our desire to be like such a tree? As the tree's roots go down deeply to receive life-giving water and nutrients, do we seek our nourishment from the life-giving word of God? Just as the tree produces flowers and fruit, are we letting the word of God guide our thinking, our attitudes and our actions, producing his fruit in us (Galatians 5:22)? Just as the tree is alive and life-giving, is the life of God coursing through us and being available to others?

Prayer

Father God, thank you for your word—wise and life-giving—through which you speak and shape us. Give us hearts that truly delight in you and your word. Like trees that live through seasonal changes and the storms that batter them, may we be people who remain rooted in you. Amen.

Reflection 2:
The Land is Mine

Background

This drone photo shows part of the extensive (2,500 ha) Burraghihnbihng wetlands (Hexham Swamp), located in Awabakal Country near Mulubinba (Newcastle). Its unique ecosystem has a diversity of plants, aquatic animals, crustaceans and migratory birds, along with fresh water supplies and was able to sustain large populations of Indigenous Australians for thousands of years.[9]

Unlike some of the early colonisers, for whom the land was an object to be tamed and exploited for material gain, the interdependence between Aboriginal and Torres Strait Islander peoples and the land is based on respect. While the land sustains and provides for the people, people manage and sustain the land through culture and ceremony.[10] From an early age, each person is entrusted with the cultural knowledge and responsibility to care for the land with which they identify through kinship systems. '*We recognised that the land had limited resources and so when we did farm, cultivate and collect food, we always made sure to only take what we needed and nothing more. We had sophisticated practices to allow the land to replenish itself of what we had taken*'.[11]

The relationships between Indigenous people and their Country are captured in their sayings such as '*healthy country, healthy people*' and '*if you look after the Country, the Country will look after you*'.[12] In caring for Country today, traditional practices relevant to land and water management are being adopted. One example is traditional Aboriginal owners sharing their cultural river management knowledge with governments to help revive Coombool Swamp near the South Australian border. Environmental water flows (a normal feature in the past) have been re-instated, and, as a result, the vegetation and wildlife are returning.[13]

Reflection

Indigenous peoples' respect for and care of the land reflected their understanding that the land did not belong to them. While the context is quite different, a similar idea is expressed in the Old Testament:

> In this Year of Jubilee everyone is to return to their own property. If you sell land to any of your own people or buy land from them, do not take advantage of each other. … The land must not be sold permanently, **because the land is mine** and you reside in my land as foreigners and strangers. Throughout the land that you hold as a possession, you must provide for the redemption of the land. (Leviticus 25:13-14, 23-24)

The 25th chapter of the ancient book of Leviticus gives explicit instruction about a year of rest, remembrance and release. It reveals the importance in God's eyes of justice for people, creatures and the land.

It is interesting that, in Verse 23, God is recorded as stating, '*the land is mine*'. The land referred to is that which was promised to the Israelites—the land of Canaan. On many occasions, the Israelites are told they are '*to take possession of*' (Deuteronomy 11:8) or will be '*entering to take over*' this land (Deuteronomy 11:10). It would be easy to read this as meaning 'to own'; however, Verse 23 in Chapter 25 of Leviticus clearly shows that Israel will possess the land as tenants. Many years ago, we moved into a house that came with the work my husband would be doing. We could live in it as if it were ours, but it belonged to another. That being the case, we tried to be ever so careful in looking after it.

Are the words in Leviticus relevant for us living on land and in homes that we have bought or are leasing? Certainly, the legal document that is evidence of our having purchased our land or rented our accommodation has legitimacy in our world, but as believers in God, we ultimately sit under a higher authority: the One who created this world. Perhaps this means considering 'the land' more thoughtfully. If God is the owner of the land on which I live, on which my community is built and which constitutes my country, then should we consider him in decisions about how to use it and what to do with it?

That God is a God of justice is very clear from the beginning of the Old Testament to the end of the New Testament. He cares about righting injustice. He wants the oppressed, the landless, the widows, the orphans and the homeless cared for and shown respect, and he wants the land given its due rest, too. This should affect what is done with the land, as there are inevitable repercussions. Is it justice to rip up forest to extract resources from below the earth and, in the process, contaminate the water and soil, thereby endangering the livelihoods and lives of local communities? Is it justice to not restore the land once the extraction of valuable resources has ended? Is it justice to consume thoughtlessly and add to the vast amounts of waste that enter landfill, contributing to land and water pollution? There are so many questions if we rightly view the land as belonging to God and view ourselves as gifted with temporary residency and responsibility to use it wisely and well.

Prayer

Father God, forgive us for seeing the world as our own. Viewing the world as yours cannot but change the way we use it. Father, show us how to be just in our use of resources and how we live. Please guide our government leaders in their decision-making, too. Amen.

Reflection 3:
Listening

Background

Who has not been delighted by a chorus of warbling magpies or the tree-top tinkling of bell miners or been charmed by the repeated high pitched piping of one of Australia's tiniest birds, the spotted pardalote (photographed opposite)?

It is generally agreed there are two main types of bird sounds: songs and calls. While not a rigid rule, songs are usually more complex and carry a clear pattern, while calls tend to be shorter and simpler and often just one syllable.[14] Furthermore, melodious songs are often used for mating and noting territory, whereas calls may be used as a piercing alarm or to warn of nearby danger.

A well-known example of birdsong in Australia is the beautiful sounds made by the superb lyrebird (*Menura novaehollandiae*). It sings, like no other bird, with an incredible mating repertoire. About 80% of its song consists of the expert mimicry of other birds (up to 25 species) and sounds (e.g., car alarms, dogs barking), joined together with a series of whistles and cackling notes that are used as territorial calls.[15] Author and birdwatcher, Jennifer Ackerman, vividly described her experience of hearing a powerful nearby burst of song in a forest: '*Never have I thrilled to birdsong so fluid, pure and orchestral, so packed with borrowings, as if all the songs of the rainforest were pouring from a single throat. Now I understand why this bird is called the mother of all songbirds*'.[16]

When a bird spots a potential enemy, it may give an alarm call warning others of danger and the need to take immediate evasive action. Some birds have an alarm call to specifically warn of aerial predators, while another alarm call is used for an approaching ground predator, such as a feral cat. The alarm call may not only be understood by birds of the same species but also by those of different species and even other animals.[17]

Reflection

It is such a joy to hear the various songs and calls of our diverse native birds. Very experienced birders, just by listening, can quickly identify the birds that are making the different sounds.

Listening is something God, through the writers of the Bible, often asks us to do. The Hebrew word *shema* means 'hear' or 'listen', but it does not mean to hear or listen passively, without paying attention. Rather, it means to 'listen' and 'do'—to actively listen and intentionally act on what we hear.[18] This is illustrated throughout the Bible.

In Psalm 5:3, for example, David says '*In the morning, Lord, you* **hear** *my voice; in the morning I lay my requests before you and wait expectantly*'. David acknowledges that God not only hears, but he is confident God will act. Countless people over the ages can testify to God hearing their prayer and acting—not necessarily within a human timeframe but according to his wisdom and timing.

Just as God hears and acts, he expects the same of his people. In Matthew 7:24-27, Jesus, by way of illustration, compares the consequences of listening and doing with listening and not doing.

> *Therefore, everyone who hears these words of mine and puts them into practice is like a wise man who built his house on the rock. The rain came down, the streams rose, and the winds blew and beat against that house; yet it did not fall, because it had its foundation on the rock. But everyone who hears these words of mine and does not put them into practice is like a foolish man who built his house on sand. The rain came down, the streams rose, and the winds blew and beat against that house, and it fell with a great crash.*

Jesus concludes his very well-known (but not easily acted on) Sermon on the Mount with this strong message. To hear and not act accordingly is foolish. Interestingly, Mahatma Gandhi frequently read the Sermon on the Mount and took it to heart, acting on its teaching regarding peaceful living and non-retaliation and applying this to his non-violent protests against injustice.[19]

Likewise, James, in his New Testament letter, writes in his first chapter, '*My dear brothers and sisters, take note of this: Everyone should be quick to listen, slow to speak and slow to become angry*'. He follows this advice about being more ready to listen than to speak with, '*Do not merely listen to the word, and so deceive yourselves. Do what it says*'. In this letter and these verses, there is a message for all of us—integrity. Our lives should match what we profess to believe. This comes from 'listening'—taking what we have heard to heart and acting on it. Perhaps a reason why Christians and the church today are sometimes held in low regard is because of the disconnect between who and what we say we believe and our actions and attitudes. We should make it a practice to check if we are hearing rightly and acting with integrity on what Jesus is saying to us.

Prayer

Father God, we ask your forgiveness for the many times when we have been slow to listen and quick to speak; when we have dishonoured you by our lack of integrity. Help us, we pray, to increasingly be eager to hear your voice—in whichever ways you choose to speak—and seek your enabling to act rightly on what we hear you saying to us. Amen.

Reflection 4:
The Wisdom of a King

Background

More than half of the world's reptiles are lizards, of which one small example is the beautifully marked mesa gecko (*Diplodactylus galeatus*), photographed west of Alice Springs in Central Australia. This little gecko (up to 5.5 centimetres long) is generally found in rocky outcrops in the ranges of Central Australia.[20] Of the 2,000+ species of geckos worldwide, 194 are found in Australia. They are mostly nocturnal with soft-scaled bodies, five finger-like digits on each foot, large eyes with vertical pupils, no eyelids, and broad fleshy tongues. In the absence of eyelids, the tongue is used to lick the eye clean.[21] They may be found around insect-attracting lights in warmer areas as well as on or under tree bark and rocks.

Geckos are renowned as champion climbers, seemingly defying gravity by effortlessly gripping and scaling smooth vertical surfaces. This is explained by the shape of their toes which have flaps of skin covered in millions of tiny hair-like structures that have even smaller (approximately 0.3% the width of a human hair) spatula-shaped tips made of beta-keratin, the same hard protein that makes up scales and feathers. The tips are so small that they interact with whatever material the gecko is climbing on at a molecular level, through weak forces called van der Waals forces. The flaps, hairs and tips work together to allow gecko toe pads to not only stick firmly but also release easily and quickly without damaging surfaces. This is something human-made adhesives cannot do, which is why engineers are so keen to create materials that imitate geckoes' abilities.[22]

Despite their amazing abilities, things don't always go to plan. While we were living in South-East Asia, a surprise guest dropped in for dinner one day. We had just placed some steamed rice into each of our bowls when a house gecko, free-falling from the ceiling, landed right in the middle of our 4-year-old's serving of rice!

Reflection

One of the delights in re-reading the Bible is that it's never a case of 'been there, done that' with nothing more to be noted or learned. In re-readings, God can draw our attention to verses that we had not previously noticed and, thereby, continue to shape our thoughts and actions. The following are such verses. They reference a range of creatures and include the reptiles, of which the little gecko is a beautiful example:

> He [Solomon] spoke three thousand proverbs and his songs numbered a thousand and five. He spoke about **plant life from the cedar of Lebanon to the hyssop that grows out of walls. He also spoke about animals and birds, reptiles and fish** (1 Kings 4:32-33).

As the newly anointed king succeeding his famous father, David, Solomon felt very inadequate for the task of ruling a nation. Thus, he prayed:

> Now, Lord my God, you have made your servant king in place of my father David. But I am only a little child and do not know how to carry out my duties. Your servant is here among the people you have chosen, a great people, too numerous to count or number. So give your servant a discerning heart to govern your people and to distinguish between right and wrong. For who is able to govern this great people of yours? (1 Kings 3:7-9)

This honest prayer, uttered in dependent humility and with a clear understanding of what leadership of a nation needed more than anything (and still does), touched God's heart:

> The Lord was pleased that Solomon had asked for this. So God said to him, '… I will give you a wise and discerning heart, so that there will never have been anyone like you, nor will there ever be'. (1 Kings 3:10-12)

Accordingly, King Solomon became renowned for his God-given wisdom:

> Solomon's wisdom was greater than the wisdom of all the people of the East, and greater than all the wisdom of Egypt. He was wiser than anyone else … And his fame spread to all the surrounding nations. (1 Kings 4:30-31)

It could, therefore, have been recorded that as a wise king, Solomon spoke about riches or buildings, servant-labour or trade, peace (his reign was noted for its peace) or women (he had very many wives and concubines). However, the text of 1 Kings 4 specifically records that Solomon observed and spoke of the world of nature—plants (from the mightiest to the least), animals and the classes of birds, fish and reptiles. In his wisdom, Solomon was neither so preoccupied with his kingdom nor his assets that he could not give considerable time to observe and consider the natural world. Was he enthralled by the range of creatures that he observed and perhaps classified? In the same way that the gecko's feet amaze us, was he, too, fascinated by the structure and abilities of the creatures he pondered?

Taking to heart the example of King Solomon and spending time observing and appreciating nature—the plants and creatures—can allow gratitude and wonder to well up within us as we recognise their witness to a majestic Creator, who has brought about such great diversity in so many ecosystems. Just as King Solomon and the creatures he observed lived under the same God, we, too, share this world with an abundance of life, which is also embraced in the love of God.

Prayer

Father God, grant us your wisdom to live in ways that please you. Like Solomon, help us to be observers of your creation, to delight in it and learn from it. For your holy name's sake. Amen.

Reflection 5:
What is Happening to My World?

Background

On a cool, overcast and rainy afternoon during a bushwalking and camping trip to Mount Kaputar National Park in north-west New South Wales in late 2021, we were extremely privileged and delighted to see a number of the rare and critically endangered giant pink slugs (*Triboniophorus* sp. nov. 'Kaputar'). Documented only as recently as 2014, Mount Kaputar is the one place in the world where these invertebrates can be found, and their range is limited to a very small area of alpine forest at the top of the mountain. The slug is large (up to an enormous 20 centimetres) and bright pink, with two protruding optic tentacles and a breathing pore or pneumostome. During dry conditions, the slugs shelter under leaf litter, woody debris and loose rocks. On some rainy nights they emerge and crawl over rock outcrops and shrubs and climb tree trunks, feeding on the biofilm of microalgae, lichen and fungi growing on these surfaces.[23] Why are they such a brightly-coloured pink? No-one knows for sure, but it does help them to be well camouflaged in the leaf litter that includes reddish-pink eucalyptus leaves. It may also serve as a warning to frighten off predators![24]

In the late-2019 bushfires, the already at-risk population was decimated by an estimated 90%, with only a low number—possibly just hundreds—surviving. The main threat now is climate change, where a small rise in temperature could lead to the extinction of this species. Australian Museum Research Associate Michael Shea wrote, '*High-elevation ecosystems are considered particularly vulnerable to the effects of climate change, and Mount Kaputar is already right on the edge of what is considered a subalpine ecosystem*'.[25] Currently, this brightly-coloured slug is regarded as an iconic flagship species for the global threat to biodiversity posed by climate change.[26]

Reflection

As the science has revealed, the world of the extraordinary giant pink slug has faced and is facing some significant changes, largely brought about by bushfires and global warming. Some years ago, the awarded atmospheric physicist Sir John Houghton published his autobiography, *In the Eye of the Storm.*[27] In this book, he shares his life and faith journey. As a scientist, he undertook research that, along with that of other scientists, led to findings that expanded knowledge and provided clear evidence of what was happening to the world in terms of its rate of warming. As co-chair of the International Panel on Climate Change, he co-authored its first three reports, and, as a scientist and a man of faith, he was deeply concerned about what was happening and felt it his duty to speak out about it. He believed God cared about what human activity and behaviour were doing to the world that he brought into being.

In reading the Bible from beginning to end, we cannot but become aware of all the instances where creation/nature is referred to and in ways such that its significance to God cannot be ignored. The Old Testament, from its very beginning in Genesis 1, reverberates with references to the natural world or creation. Creation, which God declared to be '*very good*', reveals the glory of the Creator who transformed the earth from being functionless and empty to one that teemed with a variety of life.[28] The garden in Eden, with its abundant plant life, is the place where God walked (Genesis 3:8) and the environment in which people were intentionally placed (Genesis 2:15). Creation belongs to God (Psalm 24:1, 95:4-5): it praises God (1 Chronicles 16:31-33; Psalm 66:1-4, 148:3-10), it rejoices in God (Psalm 96:11-13), and God rejoices in his creation—all his works (Psalm 104:31).

In the New Testament, the apostle Paul, in his letter to the Romans (Romans 8:19-23), wrote of the strong connection between creation and humanity. Just as the human choice to disobey God adversely affected creation, so, too, will our redemption as God's children help restore creation as it shares in the freedom and glory of God's people. Verses 21 and 22 of Romans 8 reveal that creation is groaning and awaiting this release from decay and restoration to its intended condition. Indeed, we (creation and humanity) groan together (consiously or unconsciously) in longing for and anticipation of this.

In his John Stott London lecture on Creation Care, Reverend Dr Chris Wright quotes Isaiah 6:3 and explains that the structure of the Hebrew in this verse places the word 'filling' first, such that the verse actually reads '*the filling of the earth brings glory to God*'.[29] Creation, in all its fullness, abundance, biodiversity—from the smallest to the greatest, from the more bizarre (like giant, fluorescent pink slugs) to the more ordinary—order and function, reveals the glory of God on earth. Jesus brought the kingdom of God—God's rule, God's way of seeing and doing things—to this world. As his disciples, how can we live so that creation, the work of God's hands, is not diminished? How should we live so that all of creation can continue its praise to the living God?

Prayer

Reflection 6:
Three Voices

Background

The historic lighthouse on Lady Elliott Island, a coral cay (a small, usually sandy, island situated on a coral platform) in the southern Great Barrier Reef, Queensland, was first built around 1873. This human-made structure is visibly dwarfed by a part of the vast Milky Way with its dense galactic core.

Over the centuries, scientists have helped us to gain some amazing insights into the heavens. This is beautifully illustrated by what has been discovered about the Milky Way, the spiral galaxy within which our earth is located. Like other galaxies, the Milky Way is made up of over 100 billion stars, along with gas and dust, bound together by gravity.[30] Every star we see with our naked eyes is actually a part of the Milky Way, with the only object visible without a telescope outside the galaxy being the Andromeda Galaxy.[31] The diameter of the Milky Way is estimated to be at least 100,000 light-years.[32] Even if we could travel at the speed of light (300,000 kilometres per second), it would take about 25,000 years to reach the middle of the Milky Way.

Like most other large galaxies, the Milky Way has a supermassive black hole (Sagittarius A*) at its centre, which is estimated to be millions of kilometres across and have a mass 4 million times that of the sun.[33] Just as the earth moves around the sun and the sun moves in the Milky Way, the Milky Way is also in motion, moving at an estimated 2.2 million kilometres per hour![34]

Until around 1920, most astronomers believed that all the stars in the universe were a part of the Milky Way. This changed with observations by Edwin Hubble, who proved that the Milky Way was just one of many galaxies in the universe.[35] Indeed, it is now postulated that there are over 200 billion galaxies,[36] brought into being by our amazing God!

Reflection

The heavens declare the glory of God; the skies proclaim the work of his hands. Day after day they pour forth speech; night after night they reveal knowledge …
The law of the Lord is perfect, refreshing the soul …The commands of the Lord are radiant, giving light to the eyes …
By them [God's decrees] your servant is warned; in keeping them there is great reward. But who can discern their own errors? Forgive my hidden faults.
(Psalm 19:1-2, 7, 8, 11-12)

This beautiful psalm, of which CS Lewis wrote, '*I take this to be the greatest poem in the collection of Psalms and one of the greatest lyrics in the world*',[37] expresses so clearly and eloquently the ready communication of God to humankind and the human response to his voice.

In this poem-song, God's first voice is his creation. The psalm writer, David (aka King David), as a shepherd in his youth, would have spent time guiding his flock to pasture by day and camping with them on cold nights. He would not only have lain in the darkness, awed by the immensity of the night skies (that still look down on us today) but would also have woken to the warmth of the sun signalling a new day. As such, he could readily testify to the heavens being God's universal speech and knowledge broadcast to and for the whole world to 'read'—silent speech heard by the ones who '*have ears to hear*' and read as evidence of '*God's eternal power and divine nature*' (his creative power, his ongoing goodness, faithfulness and supreme authority). This knowledge of God is available to all; but not all choose to embrace it or respond to it—do we allow '*the heavens*' and the other works of creation to speak to us of God?

This psalm goes on to acknowledge a second voice—that of '*the law*', '*the statutes*', '*the precepts*' and '*the commands*' of God. For the psalm writer, this was the Torah, the books of the law, but more rightly understood as all of God's guidance for right living. The psalm writer's personal experiences and absolute thankfulness for the guiding wisdom in the written word of God sing out from this psalm. For us today, the written word is more extensive, found in the whole Bible. Have we, like David, experienced the words from God, not as restrictive and legalistic, but rather as graciously guiding and freeing—returning us to God, giving us wisdom in our naivety, filling our hearts with joy and enlightening our thinking and the way we walk in this world?

On hearing and reading God's first and second voices, the writer responds, giving us the 'third voice' in this psalm. His response is both reflective and humble: in taking on board the warnings and guidance in '*the law of the Lord*', he is led to realise our human tendency to '*not see the plank in our own eyes*'—to be blind to our own faults and to have a propensity to intentionally resist God and rebel against his guidance. As an example to us all, he expresses his longing not to be like that.

Prayer

Great and glorious God, thank you that you speak to us from your creation, from your Word and through your servants throughout the ages. May all your 'speech' shape us, and may the words that come out of my mouth that others hear and the meditations of my heart that you see be pleasing in your sight, Lord God, Creator and Redeemer. Amen.

Reflection 7:
Do Not Touch

Background

Australia is well known for having some of the world's most venomous creatures but is lesser known for its poisonous flora that can inflict intense pain. This photograph, taken in a Hunter Valley rainforest, New South Wales, shows one such example—leaves of the giant Australian stinging tree (*Dendrocnide excelsa*) which can grow as high as 40 metres. Stinging trees are particularly well-adapted for the early colonisation of disturbed areas of rainforest, for example, after a landslide.

The extremely painful sting, which originates from the harmless-looking very fine hairs on the leaves and stems (including on fallen leaves that have been dead for months), usually lasts for several hours or days, with possible painful flares recurring for weeks or even months. The silicon hairs are needle-sharp hollows filled with a range of toxins. When touched, they act like miniature hypodermic needles by embedding themselves in the skin and delivering their toxin. The excruciating pain has been described by a PhD student studying these trees as, '*The worst kind of pain you can imagine—like being burnt with hot acid and electrocuted at the same time*'. [38]

A team from the University of Queensland's Institute for Molecular Bioscience has recently discovered, in the leaves of these trees, a completely new class of neurotoxin proteins that they termed 'gympietides', after the Indigenous name for the plant. These neurotoxins act in a similar way to spider and cone snail toxins. The researchers hope that the gympietides will provide new information on how pain works and can contribute to the development of new, more effective pain treatments.

Interestingly, despite being protected by their hairs, the leaves of stinging trees are regularly attacked by insects. For some reason, even though the toxic hairs are completely eaten in the process, there is no evidence that they cause harm to the predator.

Reflection

A warning not to touch the giant stinging tree alerts us to a danger we may have been unaware of, and, in heeding it, we are protected from an intensely painful experience. Generally, society functions effectively because there are many rules in place designed to warn us of danger and safeguard our well-being. For example, a fence and signs near a cliff edge create an intentional barrier and warn us away from unsafe surfaces and potentially deadly falls. Similarly, a 40-kilometre per hour speed limit with associated flashing red circles on the signage alerts us (when our thoughts may well be elsewhere) to school zones. These warnings and restrictions are very much appreciated because they create a safer zone when movement is at a peak and the likelihood of accidents is greater.

Undoubtedly, the effective functioning of society depends on rules and warnings such as these. The body of Christ, made up of people at all stages of their walk with Jesus, is also given two main laws or 'rules' by Jesus—'*love the Lord your God with all your heart, mind and soul and love your neighbour as yourself*' (Matthew 22:37). When we are re-birthed by God, he moves these 'laws' from being external requirements, impossible to fulfil and even provoking resistance, to '*put[ting his] laws into our hearts and writ[ing] them on [our] minds*' (Hebrews 10:16). As a result, our desires change to wanting to embrace these laws and live them out. Just as humankind made in the image of God generally lives according to an inbuilt moral compass, as followers of Jesus, our hearts are 'softened' and increasingly and gladly aligned with his way and will.

But this is not always clearcut and straightforward. In the relatively young Corinthian church, Paul was faced with attitudes that were governed by social mores that did not necessarily promote the healthy growth of the body of Christ. Some of the Corinthians in the church believed they had '*the right to do anything*' (1 Corinthians 10:23) because they were free in Christ. However, for the sake of the whole church, Paul had to remind them that '*not everything is beneficial, not everything is constructive*' (1 Corinthians 10:23). In other words, just as external rules are usually designed for the benefit of all in a society or community, Paul was advising the Corinthians to think not just of themselves but of the whole church and whether their individual attitudes or behaviours would benefit others or be a stumbling block.

Perhaps it is not something that we think much about—whether what we do or how we live causes others, particularly younger Christians, to falter in their walk or to be led down an unhelpful path. Paul explained how he makes life choices based not on what he could freely do but on what would build up others. This may, in fact—and in Paul's case, does—involve letting go of some freedoms and being seemingly restricted by the concerns of others. However, he does this because he is living out '*loving his neighbour as himself*' and therefore advises, '*no one should seek their own good, but the good of others*' (1 Corinthians 10: 24). 'Do not touch' may still be relevant but, rather than being an external imposition, is generated from within in the interests of others; both have their place in our lives.

Prayer

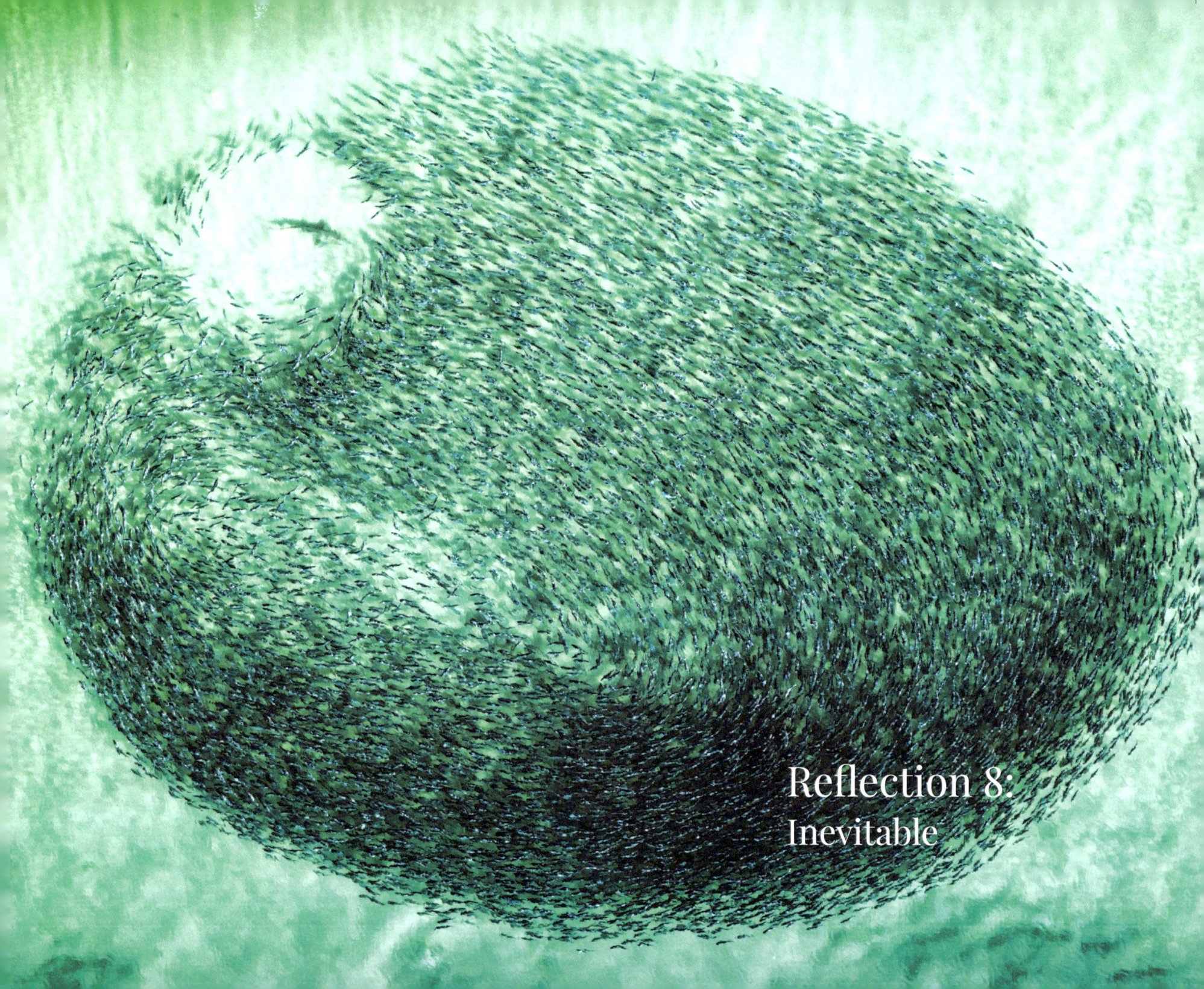

Reflection 8:
Inevitable

Background

Do you see what is happening in this 'fingerprint-like' photograph? It was taken with a drone near a surfing beach on the Central Coast, New South Wales. The fish are large eastern Australian salmon (*Arripis trutta*), while the much larger predator in the upper left-hand side is a 2.5- to 3-metre grey nurse shark (*Carcharias taurus*). While watching the unfolding scene from above, it was not uncommon to see the shark successfully find its morning meal. Death is inevitable for all animals regardless of lifespan, which may only be the brief 24 hours of adult mayflies or the hundreds of years for the bowhead whale.[39]

Death is also inevitable for all people but may come sooner rather than later, depending on the range of factors that influence life expectancy in various parts of the world. Overall, since the 19th century, life expectancies have significantly increased, largely due to reductions in infant mortality and improved health. In the early 1800s, no country in the world had a life expectancy greater than 40 years.[40] Today, the life expectancy of most people in the world is 72.6 years—similar to what it was for people in the very richest countries in 1950. This is expected to increase further to 77.1 years by 2050.

While considerable progress has been made in reducing the gap in life expectancy between and within countries, nevertheless, large differences remain. Life expectancy at birth in the least developed countries lags 7.4 years behind the global average, due largely to persistently high levels of child and maternal mortality, as well as other factors, such as violence and conflict.[41] However, regardless of where we live, the reality and often the fear of death is ever-present in our world, and recent events have brought this home in more vivid ways.

Reflection

Regardless of whether it ends a short life or comes peacefully to conclude a long life, death gives rise to many emotions: sorrow, loss, grief, pain and suffering. And these are normal human responses because losing someone we love is like losing part of oneself. Even the deaths of those we don't know personally can upset us. But is death how it was meant to be? Is this what God intended for us when he created us in his image?

The intended state of humankind was life—life brimming over with joy and vitality. The couple in the garden of Eden had unrestricted access to food from the tree of life (Genesis 2:16, 17). God created them to live a good life as part of and in his good creation. But things worked out very differently; as a consequence, death comes sooner or later to each of us.

Recently, a candid but sensitive program on television[42] looked at death and included interviews with people who were facing the reality of passing away. One of these, a lady whose death from cancer was imminent, stated, '*The most frightening part of it is that I have no idea what's going to happen*'.

God knows death, which challenges, threatens and takes life, can be the most frightening thing that each of us faces. However, in deep love and with great power, he has dealt with death and goes out of his way to tell us, as his children, what's going to happen. Why? So that we can not only know what to expect but also face death with genuine hope; so that we can be totally assured that death is not the full-stop at the end of life; so that we do not have to face it with fear (Hebrews 2:14-15).

In the above-mentioned program, it was stated, '*Hope is the chink in the curtain that lets the light through*'. God provides the basis for hope that is real and peace-bringing. In his lavish love for the world, he sent his son to deal with the root cause of death: sin. By his own death, Jesus ensured that, in its entirety, sin was dealt with justly. Then, by powerfully raising Jesus from death, God shows that both sin and death have been overcome. Through Jesus, the way through the decay and death of this world to a resurrected life beyond death has been provided. Prior to his own death, and to dear friends whose brother had died, Jesus declares, '*I am the resurrection and the life. The one who believes in me will live, even though they die; and whoever lives by believing in me will never die. Do you believe this?*' (John 11:25-26)

Death has been wonderfully defeated. This is why Paul can write, '*Death has been swallowed up in victory*' (1 Corinthians 15:54)—the victory accomplished by Jesus's death and resurrection. Death need no longer be regarded and feared as the annihilation of life.

Rather, for the child of God and follower of Jesus, by whom and through whom sin is forgiven, death, when and however it comes, will be a doorway to ongoing life in the presence of God in the reality of his unopposed kingdom of light and love.

But this does mean that the choices we make in this life do count for later.

Prayer

Thank you, Lord Jesus, that you have conquered death and are alive. Thank you that not only are you the resurrection and true life, but by your own resurrection you give us hope that can look to beyond the grave. Help us to live this life, making it count for you. Amen.

Reflection 9:
Light

Background

Have you ever heard the expression, '*light is life*'? A world without light is difficult to imagine. Light is indeed essential to life on earth.

The electromagnetic spectrum is the term used by scientists to describe the entire range of light that exists. When we think of light, we probably think of what our eyes can see. However, this 'visible' light that can be detected by the human eye is just a very small part of the electromagnetic spectrum that surrounds us. From radio waves to gamma rays, most of the light in the universe is invisible to us![43] It has the properties of both a wave (like the ripples from a pebble dropped into a pond) and a particle (photons, the most basic or elementary unit of light).[44]

Light is one of the most critical elements in a process that feeds the biosphere. On land, this usually starts with tiny chloroplasts that are found in plants and some algae. The chloroplasts capture sunlight and convert the light energy into chemical energy, which is stored as organic compounds like glucose. This capture and conversion of light to chemical energy is known as photosynthesis and is critical in nourishing most of the living world, either directly (for herbivores like elephants, koalas and cattle) or indirectly (for omnivores or carnivores like lions and eagles). The chloroplasts, which number thousands in just one leaf and contain the light-absorbing pigment chlorophyll, can be viewed as micro-chemical factories powered by the sun.

In the photograph opposite, the hundreds of seabirds (mainly common noddy, *Anous stolidus*) busily feeding at sunset in the southern Great Barrier Reef are dependent on this conversion of light energy by chloroplasts. In this case, it is the chloroplasts in microalgae (phytoplankton) that form the basis of the marine food web. They are eaten by primary consumers like zooplankton, small fish and crustaceans, which, in turn, are preyed upon by the birds.[45]

Reflection

Light is a precious thing—be it the light of the sun that brightens the sky, warms the earth and promotes plant germination and growth or the light of a torch that lessens the blackness of a dark cave or tunnel, revealing obstacles to be avoided and safer pathways to take. Many of us are drawn to light or places that are lit, and we often feel less comfortable in dark environments, where our first instinct is to turn on a light or open the blinds to let in the light.

Jesus gets this. In John's gospel, he is recorded as making the very bold claim:

I am the light of the world. Whoever follows me will never walk in darkness but will have the light of life.
(John 8:12)

This statement is bold because, first, it implies that the world apart from Jesus is in darkness. There is much that is beautiful in this world, but unfortunately, we don't need to look far to see that it has been and can be a very dark place. Throughout history, the darker side of human nature—lust and greed for power, control, wealth, land or resources (including people), along with jealousy, hatred, bitterness and revenge—has had (and continues to have) devastating effects on nations, peoples, individuals and the earth. Darkness has taken hold in the church as well, for example, in terrible cases of child abuse. On an individual level, as we examine our thoughts, desires, reactions, inactions or selfish acts, we see that we are flawed creatures. Darkness is real in so many ways and in so many places.

Just as sunlight or a lamp dispels darkness and reveals what it has been hiding, in his stunning claim to be '*the light of the world*', Jesus declares that he can dispel the darkness in this world and the darkness in our hearts. '*Whoever follows me will never walk in darkness but will have the light of life*'. As we let him in, he will shine his light on our darkness (in whatever ways he knows we can handle at particular times in our lives) and reveal what has been hidden, perhaps to ourselves but also that which we hide from others. Through his word, through prayer, through the insights of others and through the convicting work of the Holy Spirit, Jesus shows us what needs to be released or removed for our darkness to be replaced by his transforming light.

Moreover, in the same way that sunlight enables plants to grow and light shows us a path, Jesus (light) will transform our lives and guide us if we follow him. In fact, he promises we '*will never walk in darkness*'. This is truly a relief! Through the light of his words, the Spirit of truth and his presence in all the circumstances of our lives, Jesus can grow us, bringing us to maturity as members of the body of Christ.

As the light that is Jesus increasingly shines within us, our desire is increasingly to do as he instructs and '*let [our] light so shine before people that they may see [our] good works and glorify [our] father in heaven*'. In recognising that our light is the light of Jesus, like John the Baptist, we, too, must acknowledge that 'I (the parts of me that resist God) must decrease, and he (Jesus) must increase'.

Prayer

Our Creator God and Father in heaven, thank you for the light that blesses this world. Lord Jesus, may your light increasingly dispel the darkness in this world and each day, increasingly shine in each of us who follow you to bring you glory. Amen.

Reflection 10:
Humility

Background

Does a particular animal come to mind when you look at the photograph opposite? Maybe it becomes clearer when you know that this flower belongs to a group of orchids known as donkey orchids. The two larger lateral petals look like two ears of a donkey and, when these move in the wind, resemble a donkey moving its head and braying. This species is *Diuris alba* (white donkey orchid) and was growing in bushland at Doyalson, New South Wales. It is one of over 600 species of terrestrial orchids that grow in Australia, most of which are not found elsewhere.[16] Terrestrial orchids outnumber the much better-known epiphytic orchids that grow on trees and rocks.

Most terrestrial orchids are deciduous and have a growth cycle in which they spend up to 6 months as dormant underground tubers. This helps them survive during the hot and dry conditions so common in Australia. The tubers have been used as a food source by Indigenous Australians. Like many plants, they do not live independently but team up with a root fungus to form a beneficial relationship. The fungus provides carbohydrates to help the orchid seeds germinate and also feed the plant.

They are also dependent on relationships with a diversity of insects for cross-pollination and to complete their life cycle. To do this, they use a wide variety of complex, highly specialised methods. These include nectar rewards to attract the insect pollinator to the flower; deception, where the flower may resemble a female of a particular insect species and hence attract a male to mate with the flower (and, in the process, pollen attaches to the insect); and traps, which when triggered, transfer pollen to the insect.[17]

Despite being a fascinating part of the natural world, these small, mostly delicate orchids with their short flowering period are readily overlooked.

Reflection

In Western culture, the word 'humility' is sometimes regarded negatively: for some, it suggests weakness, subservience and being downtrodden. But are these what humility really is? Are our ideas shaped by our culture? What is God's view?

The God who says, '*I don't think the way you think. The way you work isn't the way I work*' (*The Message*, Isaiah 55:8) has a different view of the attitudes and values seen as important in this world. Rather than people 'getting what they deserve', God is merciful and lavishes forgiveness on those who, in sincerity, turn to him regardless of background. The act of turning to God is one of humility; it is an acknowledgement of our inadequacy and taintedness. It is also an acknowledgement of our need of God, not as a crutch to support our own way of living, but as the One who loves us and who, as our Creator, has the right and wisdom to guide our lives. This is one example of humility.

In the Galilean town of Nazareth, a young, unmarried woman, Mary, was unexpectedly visited by an angel, whose words '*Greetings, you who are highly favoured! The Lord is with you*' (Luke 1:28) disturbed her and set her wondering. The angel proceeded to give her more mind-blowing information—that, in her virginal state, she would become pregnant by the power of the Holy Spirit with a baby who would be a king! And Mary's response? '*I am the Lord's servant,*' ... *May your word to me be fulfilled*' (Luke 1:38). Mary, engaged to be married to a man named Joseph, did not ask for this visitation or honour. To become pregnant under such circumstances would be highly dishonourable and likely to draw much censorship. However, what stands out is Mary's humility. In her willingness to surrender to what God was doing, she was not only accepting the certain joy of having a child but also the pain and grief of a mother whose son would not only be loved but also misread, rejected and horribly crucified.

Jesus, in turn, as the One '*[whose] kingdom will never end*' (Luke 1:33), shows the world what kingship is like God's way. It is a life of true humility and service. Jesus let go of his rights and seat at God's right hand, and '*being found in appearance as a man, he humbled himself, by becoming obedient to death— even death on a cross*' (Philippians 2:8)! He let go of heaven and entered a world tainted by sin in every respect; he let go of equality with God to accept the limitations of a human body, needing sleep, food and shelter. For his 3 years of ministry, he served—teaching, healing, restoring life and revealing God. On his much hailed entry into Jerusalem—so unlike that of any Roman leader who would have displayed his victory by parading on a powerful white stallion—Jesus rode into the city on the back of a young donkey. He embodied humility in every respect—relinquishing his rights as God and undergoing deep suffering to serve God the Father and execute his rescue plan for the world.

Humility is seeing clearly where we really stand under God and recognising our dependence on him for re-birth into his family and ongoing life in his kingdom; humility is not weakness but boldly accepting the roles God gives us at different times in our lives and which may require a lot of strength and courage. Humility is not subservience but rather being willing to serve others in love (with or without recognition), knowing it is God's way to live in this world.

Prayer

Lord Jesus, help us not to think of ourselves more highly than we should, but with sound assessment and in humility to consider others better than ourselves. Amen.

Reflection 11:
The Mighty Sea

Background

Taken at Frazer Beach (Munmorah State Conservation Area), this photograph captures a large breaking wave in the big swell generated by the Tongan earthquake.

We live on a blue planet, with oceans and seas up to 11,000 metres deep covering more than 70% of its surface. In recent decades, awareness of the critical role of the world's oceans and seas and our dependence upon their status has increased. For example, it has been estimated by scientists that 50% to 80% of the oxygen production on earth, which is vital for both marine and terrestrial life, comes from the ocean, the world's largest ecosystem. This is mainly produced by oceanic plankton, drifting plants, algae and some photosynthesising bacteria.[48] The oceans absorb heat from the sun, reduce the impact of global warming and help regulate our climate and weather patterns. They play a key role in the water cycle, without which most of the planet would be desert, as well as provide food for vast numbers of people, along with a range of medicinal products including ingredients that help fight cancer, arthritis, Alzheimer's disease and heart disease.[49,50] Most of us have likely also been inspired by the beauty and ever-changing moods of the sea as well as having enjoyed it for recreations, such as swimming, snorkelling, fishing or surfing. The oceans also serve as the foundation for much of the world's economy, supporting sectors from tourism to fisheries to international shipping.

While seas are of critical importance and often appear calm and mesmerizing, they can also be dangerous, causing massive destruction and erosion. We were involved in some work in Aceh, Indonesia after the 2004 Indian ocean earthquake and associated tsunami. Working in a city not far from the epicentre, we saw the traumatic impact of the 25-metre waves that led to the deaths of 30,000 people in just this one location.

Reflection

The sea features in several of the Bible's accounts. Genesis 1 tells of God's speaking creation into being, including, ' "Let the water under the sky be gathered to one place, and let dry ground appear." And it was so. God called the dry ground "land," and the gathered waters he called "seas." And God saw that it was good' (Genesis 1:9-10). The sea, in its place, was 'good'. However, in the world of the Israelite people, the sea was often regarded as threatening:

The seas have lifted up, Lord, the seas have lifted up their voice; the seas have lifted up their pounding waves. Mightier than the thunder of the great waters, mightier than the breakers of the sea—the Lord on high is mighty. (Psalm 93:3-4)

These verses in Psalm 93:3-4 depict the potentially destructive power of the sea—its rising up, its thunderous noise, its mighty waves. Yet, the writing does not stop there. The psalmist continues. Far greater than the seemingly irrepressible power of the waves is God, who created the sea. This is exemplified in the Israelites' crossing of the Red Sea in their escape from Egypt, where they had lived in slavery:

Then Moses stretched out his hand over the sea, and all that night the Lord drove the sea back with a strong east wind and turned it into dry land. The waters were divided, and the Israelites went through the sea on dry ground, with a wall of water on their right and on their left. (Exodus 14:21-22)

Using the force of the wind that was already in the system he had created, God transformed the sea from being an obstacle to the people's flight to becoming a pathway to freedom.

Hundreds of years later, during his ministry in Galilee, Jesus decided to cross the Sea of Galilee in a boat with his disciples. A savage squall arose, and waves threatened to swamp the boat. The disciples, despite some of them having earnt their living as fishermen on the lake, were terrified and roused their sleeping teacher, Jesus, to help them. As the agent through which 'all things were made [and] without [whom] nothing was made that has been made' (John 1:3), Jesus acted authoritatively. 'He got up, rebuked the wind and said to the waves, "Quiet! Be still!" Then the wind died down and it was completely calm' (Luke 8:22-24). An amazing transformation took place! The sea, potentially life-threatening, was responsive to the control of the One through whom it was made.

As a young girl, I nearly drowned at a local beach. Swamped by waves, I was struggling to surface while my non-swimmer mother, watching from the shore, frantically called for help. Suddenly, a stranger lifted me up out of the water and restored me to my grateful parent. Perhaps this experience engendered in me a strong fear of the ocean. So, what do these texts say? My fear has now mostly been replaced by a healthy respect— the sea, after all, can be very dangerous. However, rather than watch a wild sea with just fear, I can now look beyond it to the God who is greater than its restless energy and seething power, who is the Creator of the beauty of the ocean and all the life in it and who is more than able to bring peace to any storms in my life.

Prayer

Almighty God, you are Lord over all creation, of which the sea is a truely amazing part. We also acknowledge that disasters occur which are beyond our understanding. In our helplessness, we look to you to make a way through and bring peace to what seems out-of-control in our lives. Amen.

Reflection 12:
Soaring Like an Eagle

Background

Have you been intrigued watching the different flight patterns of birds—an eagle soaring across a valley, a flock of shorebirds swirling over mudflats or swallows darting through the air after insects.

Eagles are perfect examples of what it means to effortlesly climb high into the sky against the forces of gravity. Australia has several large eagle species including the white-bellied sea-eagle (*Haliaeetus leucogaster*), photographed near Newcastle, New South Wales, at an estuary searching for food. Like most other eagles, sea eagles have long, large wings, a short neck and legs short enough to tuck into their body while flying. Their long wings are wide enough to carry their own body weight plus the weight of most of the fish they prey upon.

While eagles require considerable energy to take off, they can fly long distances and reach heights of over 3,000 metres with minimal effort, primarily by soaring and gliding.[51] Instead of flapping their wings as they do to take off, they instead rely on rising air currents to gain and maintain altitude. Even though they are capable of sustained flapping flight, they may spend just several minutes per hour doing this while searching for food far below.[52] One type of rising air current is the thermal updraft, formed when energy from the sun heats the surface air, causing it to rise. Eagles can efficiently circle within the rising air columns to gain height and then glide out of the thermal updraft to move with ease across the landscape.[53] Air updrafts can also form when winds are deflected upward by ridges or hills. Eagles can use these updrafts to soar at relatively lower altitudes across the terrain.

Both of these are great examples of energy conservation, with the eagles using the updrafts generated from the sun's energy to move effortlessly across the land.[54]

Reflection

It is hard to observe an eagle majestically soaring in apparent freedom and not be captivated by the sight. Such an image is used in Chapter 40 in the book of the prophet Isaiah, which records words addressed to the Israelites who had been taken into exile in Babylon.

The Lord is the everlasting God, the Creator of the ends of the earth. He will not grow tired or weary, and his understanding no one can fathom. He gives strength to the weary and increases the power of the weak. Even youths grow tired and weary, and young men stumble and fall; but those who hope in the Lord will renew their strength. **They will soar on wings like eagles; they will run and not grow weary, they will walk and not be faint.** (Isaiah 40:28-31)

In the preceding Verses 12-26, vivid imagery and poetic language portray the incomparable greatness and supremacy of God over creation and throughout history and, therefore, over and above the gods and idols in Babylon competing for the Israelites' attention and worship.

Verse 27 acknowledges that God's people feel that it is pointless to hope in God and have questioned whether he really does see or even care about what they are going through ('*Why do you continue to complain, Jacob? Why do you say, Israel, "My way is hidden from the Lord; my cause is disregarded by my God"?*'). Isaiah assures them that contrary to their despondent thinking, God does care and will rescue them from exile, which he is more than able to do (and he did do so in an extraordinary way).

In the concluding verses of Chapter 40, Isaiah reminds the people of the eternal nature of God, of his being so far beyond the limitations that constrain humankind and creation—limitations related to vitality and perseverance and to time and knowledge. People age: we grow weary and become weak—not just the elderly among us but also young people run out of steam. God doesn't: his power is beyond our imagination as is his understanding. We cannot know the future or at times understand why we must wait (and keep waiting) for the change or relief that we have prayed for. God can and does understand. In today's world, technology has accustomed us to things happening, if not instantaneously, then very quickly. We easily become impatient when our timetables are not met, but God has a very different view of time as well as knowledge of what transformation can and may need to take place in the waiting.

It is an act of faith to submit to God's wisdom and timing and to depend on him for strength and enabling when reality appears to dictate otherwise. Trust him, says Isaiah, wait for him—not in a resigned way, but with expectation, and, in your weakness and frailty, let him be your strength. Let him be the updraft that takes you, not out of your infirmity necessarily, but that lifts you up with it to soar like an eagle. The power of this image is in the contrast: on the one hand, defeated by a sense of hopelessness and the belief that God is too far from us to care; on the other, looking to God in trust and in his time, lifted within our circumstances to a freedom and energy graciously given by God himself. It is an image of a transformation powered by God and beyond understanding.

Prayer

Lord God, mighty in wisdom and power, thank you that we need not be bound by our human frailty. Thank you that your strength is made perfect in our weakness when we look beyond ourselves and put our hope in you. Amen.

Reflection 13:
Forest in the City

Background

People in Newcastle, New South Wales, are fortunate to live in a city with two large areas of forest within or adjacent to the urban environment. This photograph shows a part of Glenrock State Conservation Area, which stretches along the coastline and is surrounded on three sides by suburbs. It is within the traditional country of the Awabakal people and contains remnant vegetation representative of the area as well as over 145 cultural and historic sites.[55] It is greatly appreciated and heavily accessed by locals and both national and international visitors.

While the need for green spaces in cities is widely recognised, Joni Mitchell's lyrics '*They paved paradise. And put up a parking lot*',[56] still ring true. As urbanisation has rapidly increased around the world (e.g., 86% of all Australians now live in an urban environment),[57,58] communities are appreciating the value of forests and other green spaces in their cities. This has been highlighted by their increased use during the recent pandemic and by research looking at the social, health, environmental and economic impacts.[59,60]

Urban forests not only have many environmental benefits, such as providing habitat refuges, but can also contribute to improving health by filtering air and water in cities where air pollution and water management may pose public health risks.[61] Furthermore, there is evidence that proximity to green spaces, even tree-lined streets, is correlated with physical and psychological well-being.[62]

Interestingly, the green spaces of city parklands have also been assessed as providing an economic benefit that can be much greater than the initial investment and ongoing maintenance costs. This is achieved through increased tourism revenue to local businesses, decreased medical costs through healthier communities, increase in land value and attractiveness, reduced urban heating, lower storm water treatment costs and positive impacts on global warming.[63]

Reflection

Then the angel showed me the river of the water of life, as clear as crystal, flowing from the throne of God and of the Lamb down the middle of the great street of the city. On each side of the river stood the tree of life, bearing twelve crops of fruit, yielding its fruit every month. And the leaves of the tree are for the healing of the nations. (Revelation 22:1-2)

An early chapter of the Bible (Genesis 2) provides a description of a garden (Eden) where humans are placed. In this green space, humankind could delight in its beauty, receive nourishment from its produce and enjoy the responsibility of looking after and cultivating it. While this garden had many trees, two are specifically named—'*the tree of life*' and '*the tree of knowledge of good and evil*'. The former was accessible; the latter was not to be eaten from. Nevertheless, Adam and Eve sought to be self-ruling and independent of God by eating from the forbidden tree of knowledge of good and evil. This brought death, decay and associated pain and suffering upon the earth. Subsequently, they were banned from eating from the tree of life, which would have perpetuated their decaying state.

At the other end of the Bible, in its very last chapter (Revelation 22), a renewed Eden is described. John, the writer of the book of Revelation, vividly records dreams and visions in dramatic and poetic language that draws heavily on Old Testament scripture and teaching. He depicts the mighty battle between evil and God, between the anti-Christ (or all that has been opposed to Christ through the ages) and God (Creator and Redeemer of life), and the eventual victory and absolute supremacy of God. He then moves to the finale—the destination of all believers who have remained true to God despite their faith being tested in so many ways. Their place of residence is no longer a pristine garden but an exquisite and unimaginably beautiful city. It is intentionally and substantially constructed with a defined boundary, suggesting a place where the international community of God's people are free to live in complete safety. This city is also described as being lit and governed by God in all his radiance, goodness, wisdom, justice, grace and power.

While this city is very different from the garden of Eden, it does share vital features—water and trees! This is a city that, far from being devoid of nature, has a life-sustaining river and trees in prime locations—'*On each side of the [life-giving] river [flowing from the throne of God and the Lamb] stood the tree of life*'. In his book, *Garden City*, JM Comer refers to the greenery in this city as 'a forest'.[64] Just as trees and forests in cities today are being shown to have significant life-enhancing benefits, so, too, will they have these when heaven comes to earth, and the curses brought about by Adam and Eve's choices in Eden are totally dealt with. Trees of life, with their life-giving and healing properties, will be accessible to all in this city. The ongoing destiny of all those from every corner of the earth who have trusted in God through the ages will be a life that is abundant and whole in the glorious presence of God and Jesus.

Prayer

Heavenly Father, we thank you for trees and forests and their wonderful benefits and for those who have enabled them to thrive in cities. We thank you, too, for the assurance that one day all your people will live with you in your presence where life and wholeness abound. Amen.

Reflection 14:
Provision

Background

Australia is home to 56 parrot species, including the brilliantly coloured Australian king-parrot (*Alisterus scapularis*), seen here feeding on seeds of an acacia (wattle) tree. Generally, parrots eat seeds, nuts, fruit, berries, flowers, nectar and pollen, with some also feeding on insects and other small prey, including invertebrate larvae, snails and grubs.[65]

As with so many creatures in our natural world, there are some fascinating stories about how some birds seek and find their food. One story that has been shared internationally is the learned behaviour of sulphur-crested cockatoos, which have been observed to cleverly prise open roadside garbage bins in search of food. These cockatoos have been filmed using their beak and foot to lift the heavy lid, then shuffling along the side to flip it over, accessing a rich reward of discarded food.[66] This suggests that the slur 'bird brain' is quite inappropriate. With their well-developed brains, some birds also use tools in their search for food. For example, the woodpecker finch on the Galapagos Islands may find and fashion a cactus spine or wooden splinter to dig grubs or other insects out of holes in cactuses.

With most Australians living in urban areas, there are several things we can do to support the provision of food for our native birds. Birdlife Australia[67] suggests that one of the best ways is to conserve and grow native shrubs and trees that provide shelter and food within our own yards and beyond.[68] If we put out food, they strongly advise against using food such as bread and mincemeat: the former is of little nutritional value and just fills the birds up, while the latter lacks nutrients that carnivorous birds would normally obtain from their natural diet and may lead to bacterial infections and other problems.[69] While there is nothing wrong with putting out very small amounts of nutritional food (e.g., seeds, nuts, berries or chopped fruit), it has been observed that the desire to do this is often more about us than the birds.[70]

Reflection

He makes springs pour water into the ravines; it flows between the mountains. They give water to all the beasts of the field; the wild donkeys quench their thirst. The birds of the sky nest by the waters; they sing among the branches. ... The trees of the Lord are well watered, the cedars of Lebanon that he planted. There the birds make their nests; the stork has its home in the junipers. (Psalm 104:10-12, 16-17)

Look at the birds of the air; they do not sow or reap or store away in barns, and yet your heavenly Father feeds them. (Matthew 6:26)

As the Creator of the universe and life on earth, God has set in place systems that have continued to sustain life over millennia. Psalm 104, in the Old Testament, celebrates the ways in which God provides for his creation. In Matthew's gospel, in the New Testament, Jesus calls us to observe birds and flowers and shows how they illustrate God's ability and faithfulness in providing not only for these but also for people.

In reading Matthew 6:26, we might simply regard it as an illustration; however, what could be otherwise glossed over—the reality of birds finding food—does speak of God. He is not a God who creates and then forgets about what he has created. As Psalm 104 indicates, he is a God who creates, nurtures, and sustains his creation for as long as it lives. Certainly, birds must work on hollows or gather nesting materials to build their homes or fly and forage to find their food, but it is God's intention that trees and food, in all their diversity, are there for them.

As people created in God's image and who have been made new creations in Christ, we have the mandate of co-ruling creation in such a way that respects and reflects God. He cares; as his children we, too, should care. We should be wiser in trying to get the balance right between development and looking after the environment and the life within it. Generally, the actions of humanity—often driven by poverty but also by a profit motive—are indeed thwarting the sustainability of God's creation. This is the case for many bird species in Australia. In many places, the trees and forests have been and are being removed at increasing rates with little regard for the long-term consequences—untold damage to the land, to biodiversity and to ecosystems. In addition to this, human-induced climate change is affecting seasonal weather patterns and the habitats where they live.

In her book, *Stewards of Eden*,[71] Sandra Richter begins her final chapter with a quotation from an interview with Gus Speth, Professor of Law at Vermont Law School, who thought that science could address the major environmental problems in the world. He concludes, however, that scientists cannot address the real causes of the environmental problems we are facing—selfishness, greed and apathy. He acknowledges that the answer is spiritual transformation—the work of God in the lives of people to enable us to live as God intended on this earth—fulfilling our mandate to reflect him in caring for the created order and each other.

Prayer

Father God, we acknowledge that, in so many ways, we work against you and not with you in the care of your creatures. Forgive us, Lord, and show us more clearly how we, beginning in our own backyards, can be co-carers with you for your glory. Amen.

Reflection 15:
Faithfulness

Background

During our trip to the Kimberley coast a few years ago, we had the privilege and delight of visiting and staying in some more remote places on Indigenous lands. One of those was Mercedes Cove, which, with its more than adequate and environmentally-friendly accommodation for visitors, was totally unspoiled by overdevelopment. As a result, the lovely natural features of the area were a highlight. On a warm afternoon in the late autumn, we walked over some dunes to this smaller cove, where we sat on the warm sand, with waves gently lapping the shore, and drank in the beauty of the setting sun. Even as I write this, I can sense the peacefulness of this place at that time.

One of the lovely aspects of camping and bushwalking is that it is easy to get into the rhythm of going down with the sun and getting up with it as it returns to bring light and warmth to a new day. Away from dense urban areas, sunrise is usually accompanied by birdsong which, together with the first light, serves as a very effective and joyful alarm clock. Dr Miriam-Rose Ungunmerr Baumann AM, the Senior Australian of the Year in 2021, captures this rhythm established by God so beautifully in her words:

My people have been so aware of nature. It is natural that we will feel close to the Creator. Our Aboriginal culture has taught us to be still and to wait. We do not try to hurry things up. We let them follow their natural course—like the seasons. We watch the moon in each of its phases. We wait for the rain to fill our rivers and water the thirsty earth. When twilight comes, we prepare for the night. At dawn we rise with the sun. We watch the bush foods and wait for them to ripen before we gather them.[72]

Reflection

In many ways, regularity is the staple of our lives. We slip into regular ways of doing things either thoughtfully or sometimes without much thought. Regularity gives us a measure of peace and security because it makes life, to some degree, predictable. This is implied in the verses in Genesis recorded after the flood, when the earth was being reinhabited by creatures and humankind. God is recorded as promising:

As long as the earth endures, seedtime and harvest, cold and heat, summer and winter, day and night will never cease. (Genesis 8:22)

That the earth will consistently turn on its axis, that the seasonal changes will occur with regularity, and that as a result, people can purposefully engage in activities that sustain life—all testify to God's goodness and faithfulness. Perhaps we take for granted these God-given systems of common grace that are predictable, provide stability and enable foreplanning.

In the same way that the consistent functioning of the earth allows for forward planning and regular activities, in his relationship with his people, God repeatedly gives them advance notice of the consequences of their choices and actions as a way of encouraging them to make wise choices. He doesn't want them to be caught unawares or to misunderstand his character or the nature of their commitment to him:

See, I set before you today life and prosperity, death and destruction. For I command you today to love the Lord your God, to walk in obedience to him, and to keep his commands, decrees and laws; then you will live and increase, and the Lord your God will bless you in the land you are entering to possess. But if your heart turns away and you are not obedient, and if you are drawn away to bow down to other gods and worship them, I declare to you this day that you will certainly be destroyed. You will not live long in the land you are crossing the Jordan to enter and possess. (Deuteronomy 30:15-18)

The people of Israel, in their relationship with God, were given laws and guidelines to live by. Obeying these would have seen them flourish and be markedly different from the nations around them, reflecting God's character. However, over time and under many leaders, the nation was led away from their God and into the very practices that they were warned against. Time and again, God, in his faithfulness to them as his chosen people, gave them the opportunity to change their minds (repent) and turn back to him. However, ultimately, their rejection of him was so thorough that the consequences, which he had so often and so clearly spoken about, were inevitable. They were attacked by the kings of other nations and forcibly taken into exile for an extended period until God opened the way for them to return to their land. In their unfaithfulness, God showed himself faithful to his word and character despite his longing for a much better outcome (Hosea 7:13).

As the One who established the systems that sustain all life in this world and brought us into being to enjoy a relationship with himself, God is ever ready to hear our cry—be it from a place of belief or even unbelief—and in goodness, grace, mercy and love turn his face to us and work within us to be the people we were intended to be. Why? Because he is faithful, not only in enabling and sustaining creation, but also in renewing and restoring life in people made in his image.

Meditation

What are the ways—in my thoughts, words and actions, in the little things and the big things—in which I can be more faithful to God who has called me and who is faithful (1 Thessalonians 5:23-24)?

Five Stories from the Natural World

The Bible—in both the Old and New Testaments, tells us clearly that creation is the work of God. It is described as being '*good, very good*'. In its diversity, beauty, abundance, complexity, life and colour it brings glory to God. It praises God. It is sustained by God. At the same time, it has been and continues to be affected by humanity's choices and actions. We are told in Genesis that when humans intentionally chose not to trust God, creation was adversely affected and stricken with decay and death. Conversely, Paul tells us in Romans that it will be released from this and renewed, sharing in freedom and glory, when all God's children are revealed. Nature or creation is integral (not incidental) to God's work in this world—from beginning to end. Indeed, both creation and salvation are the two great works of God.

The following five stories feature relationships in the natural world that are not so widely known. They shed light on interactions between creatures that are similar and those that are different, as well as interactions between creatures and their environments. Each story reveals degrees of interconnectedness and behavioural complexity. These, in turn, show how varied and intricate life is, how relatively little we know and how much more there is to be revealed, and highlight the importance of looking beyond an individual species to the ecosystem of which it is an integral part.

It is our hope that these stories will surprise you and cause you to marvel and that, as result, you will be led to both praise God and more fully appreciate the worth of these creatures and looking after the environments in which they live.

In the same way that creation is integral to God's revelation of himself, care for the earth and its life should be integral to the normal life of a Christian disciple.[73]

1. Turtle Tears and Butterflies

On a hot, humid and intermittently sunny day, imagine being in a small motorboat heading along a narrow, silt-laden tributary in the Amazon jungle. The land adjacent to the river is dense with towering rainforest. The river trip is constantly enlivened by a cacophony of sounds—birds, monkeys, insects and other unfamiliar creatures. Occasionally, there is a flash of brilliant colour, and you see a flock of macaws, their loud calls and squawks receding as they disappear into the adjacent forest. You round a bend in the river and come across a scene you have never witnessed before. On a half-submerged log resting against the bank, you see several large turtles enjoying the warmth of the sun. Busily flying around them are dozens of colourful butterflies. Some land on the reptiles' faces and even very near or on their eyes. The turtles do not seem overly disturbed by the close aerial activity as the butterflies flit from one creature to the next.

What is happening? The butterflies—and there appear to be several different species, each with their own distinctive colours and markings—are actually drinking tears released from the turtles' eyes. This phenomenon was videoed in early 2018 by Phil Torres, a tropical entomologist and science communicator, while travelling down Peru's Tambopata River.[74] He described the experience as one of the most '*bizarre, strange, beautiful, fascinating things [he had] ever seen in [his] entire life*'.

So what is the explanation? It is now understood that the diet of these butterflies, based on sugar-rich nectar, is salt-deficient and does not meet their bodies' requirement for sodium for metabolism and egg production. Though bountiful in the ocean, salt is often a rare and valuable resource on land for many insects and other animals, particularly in the western Amazon, which is over 1,500 km from the ocean. On the other hand, through their carnivorous diet, the turtles obtain more than sufficient sodium, some of which is excreted through their tears.[75] While drinking the tears has clear benefits for the butterflies, there are no known benefits for the turtles: an interesting example of commensalism—a symbiotic relationship between two species where one benefits, and the other isn't harmed.

Further observations by naturalists and others have shown that this behaviour also occurs with other insects and creatures, for example, with bees and salt-excreting animals, such as caimans.[76]

The more commonly observed insect behaviour that seems to serve a similar purpose is 'mud-puddling'. Butterflies and other species that employ this strategy will congregate around and suck up moist substances from puddles containing mineral deposits, including sodium. For many mud-puddling species, it has been observed that only males are involved, passing along salts and mud-derived nutrients to females during reproduction.[77]

2. The Ants Cut Through

Meet the amazing leaf cutter ant! In the daytime, if you were to walk through a Central or South American forest, you might see a tiny narrow trail that winds along the forest floor. Return at night-time, and you would see an incredible sight—thousands of ants marching to and fro on this 'rainforest superhighway' and along branches wherever you looked: some are heading in one direction, carrying green leaves, and others, with no leaves, are going in the opposite direction. These are leaf cutter ants that, along with humans, form one of the largest and most complex creature societies on earth.

What is happening in this image? Having left their nest, the ants are transporting leaf portions that they have cut from forest bushes and trees. In one day, they can decimate a whole tree, and, over the course of one year, they can decimate 17% of the surrounding biomass. They use their razor-sharp mandibles to slice away pieces of green leaf, with their jaw vibrating a thousand times a second in the process. When a leaf segment is free, the ant balances it in its mandibles, and returns, along with thousands of other leaf-carrying ants, to the nest, each carrying a load up to 20 times its body weight.

Back at the nest, which may extend up to half a square kilometre underground and consist of more than eight million individuals, something quite fascinating occurs. The leaves are not consumed by the ants because they are unable to break them down into digestible food. Rather, after being chewed into smaller fragments, the leaf portions are used to cultivate fungi in the nest. An estimated 2.9 kilometres of cutting with mandibles is required to reduce a square metre of leaf to fungal substrate.[78] This activity bears similarities to some of our farming practices and perhaps these ants can appropriately be called the world's first farmers.[79,80] Not only do the ants cultivate the fungi by providing it with freshly cut green leaves (fertiliser), but they also clear away decaying material and garbage and protect it from moulds and pests. They also use a bacterium that grows on their bodies and secretes antimicrobials to protect their fungi. In turn, the fungi are a food source for the ant colony.[81,82] This is a good example of mutualism—a symbiotic relationship between two living species where both benefit.

The ant colony is divided into different groups depending on function—very much a team effort! Foragers, or mediae, are the ones that cut and bring the leaf fragments back to the nest. Minors are the first line of defence, patrolling the foraging lines. Majors, or soldiers, defend the nest from intruders and are involved in trail clearing. Minims are the smallest workers that tend the fungus gardens, including collecting and transporting garbage to dedicated garbage rooms placed well below the rest of the nest. One queen rules the colony and produces larvae. The nest contains male ants only when it is ready to expand into new colonies. The winged males fly away with the fertile females but die soon after mating, having played their part in starting a new ant colony.[83]

Leafcutter ants provide an example of how a massive society can sustainably coexist, not only within their habitat but also benefiting from their taking care of it. Every job contributes to their intentional gardens and the crops of fungus they grow.[84]

3. Firestick Birds

For over 60,000 years, Australia's Indigenous communities have been caring for Country by using effective land management practices that work in with the environment. One example of this is their methods of fire management. Having long been proven to be effective, cool burning or cultural burning practices continue to be used and lately are being investigated by some state fire services. The fires burn slowly, reducing fuel loads and creating a mosaic of burnt and unburnt country. This generates patchy habitats preferred by small animals and minimises the impact of wildfires from lightning strikes.[85]

Indigenous people in Northern Australia have made observations during the fires and passed down stories of sightings that have rarely been made by non-Indigenous people, namely 'firehawks' spreading fires for food capture. This has been treated with a degree of scepticism by some non-Indigenous people, who have questioned whether birds are able to use fire as a tool.[86] The suggestion has also been made that, even if birds have been seen carrying burning sticks that have set off new fires when dropped, it may have been accidental rather than intentional.

To better understand this, Professor Mark Bonta and his colleagues from Pennsylvania State University carried out a 7-year (2011 to 2017) research project that included an examination of the literature, interviews with Indigenous people, fire rangers, academics and others who had witnessed firehawks carrying fire in Northern Australia, along with the team's own field observations.[87]

Their studies showed that at least three species—the black kite (*Milvus migrans*), whistling kite (*Haliastur sphenurus*) and brown falcon (*Falco berigora*)—often flocked in substantial numbers around grassland fires to feed on prey, such as grasshoppers and small mammals, flushed out by the flames and smoke. Very occasionally, one or more birds have been seen dropping down to seize burning sticks with their beaks or talons. These have then been carried to unburnt areas that may be up to a kilometre away, where they are released, setting these as yet unburnt areas on fire. As the new fire spreads, the birds feed on the insects and other animals driven out by the flames.

Despite the lack of unequivocal video or photographic evidence, which the researchers acknowledge would be difficult to obtain as it would require being at the fire front just at the time this somewhat rare event occurs, they concluded that: *Most accounts and traditions unequivocally indicate intentionality on the part of [the] three raptor species [mentioned above] and a handful provide evidence of cooperative fire-spreading by select individuals from within larger fire-foraging raptor assemblages.*[88] Professor Bonta and his colleagues plan to build on this study by devising a methodology to study bird behaviour right at the fire front. As uncommon as it is, they acknowledge that further research is important, as there are accounts that this practice can lead to new bushfires, making it more difficult to control a blaze.[89]

4. Wide Underground Web

Over a number of decades, we have had the privilege of walking in beautiful and diverse forests in very different regions. On these walks, we have marvelled at the surrounding scenery—the trees, bushes, wildflowers, the sun filtering through the canopy, the sounds of life and the darting brilliance of birds and butterflies. While we knew a little about what was under our feet, it has only been in recent years that we have come to a much greater appreciation of the extensive world in the soil below. This story focuses on one aspect of this life underground.

As shown in the illustration, hidden below ground level are not just tree roots but a surprisingly extensive, intertwined network of roots and white fungal mycorrhiza. In thinking of fungi, we may visualise a tasty mushroom or even a bright orange fungus on a log. However, this is just reducing fungi to one very small albeit important part of what they are—their fruiting body. The much more extensive part of a fungus is a large interwoven network of mycelium consisting of microscopically thin threads called hyphae. When growing in association with plant roots, they form a mutually beneficial relationship called a mycorrhizal network (from the Greek, *myco*, 'fungi' and *rhiza*, 'root'). To help visualise the extent of these networks—it is estimated that just a handful of forest soil may contain up to 120 kilometres of fungal hyphae![90]

While it has been said that we know more about the stars in the sky than we do about what's happening in the soil under our feet, researchers have made some fascinating discoveries in the past 30 years. One high-profile person leading the investigations into mycorrhizal networks is Canadian professor of forestry Suzanne Simard. Having spent time researching the most effective methods for growing trees with logging firms and the British Columbia Government, she came to doubt the wisdom of the prevailing approach, whereby companies cleared forests, planted rows of fast-growing trees and chopped down or killed everything else growing near them. She felt this approach ignored nature's design and what she had observed happening in nearby old-growth forests.

In a series of innovative experiments, Professor Simard discovered that trees are connected to one another through vast and complex underground fungal root mycorrhizal networks. Her research points to trees being able to share carbon, water and nutrients with other trees, including different species, and also being able to transmit information, for example, about impending threats, by sending chemical and electrical signals through the mycorrhizal network. From the tree roots, the fungi extract sugars that they use for fuel but which they cannot produce on their own—another example of mutualism between species resulting in a win-win for all. Professor Simard's doctoral research findings were published in the prestigious journal *Nature*, with the innovative front cover to the journal titled, '*The Wood Wide Web*' because of the similarities with the internet as well as neural networks.[91]

Scientists now believe all trees and many other plants benefit from a mycorrhizal network. Research continues into this fascinating area, including its broad implications for improved forest management as well as the impact of bushfires on the wide underground web.

5. The Mantas Go to the Cleaners

Moving around in the oceans are millions of tiny creatures—largely invisible to the naked eye. They include ectoparasites that, as the name suggests, exist by sucking the blood of larger sea creatures. 'Ecto'- simply means that these parasites live on the outside of other creatures. This means that the oceans are home to millions of creatures equivalent to land-based insects, like ticks and mosquitoes, that make life for humans and animals very uncomfortable and can carry the risk of disease.

In the ocean, these parasitic hitchhikers, like gnathiid isopods, branchiura and copepods, swim around looking for marine hosts on which to lodge and feed. They can have deleterious effects on their unwitting hosts. Gnathiid isopods, for example, can reduce the amount of blood circulating in the host, damage its tissue and pass on other parasitic diseases in the same way that mosquitoes pass on malaria or dengue fever to humans. Furthermore, if a particular host has large numbers of them, it can die.[92] So what is a manta ray (the feature creature in this story) to do?

Manta rays, although related to stingrays, are commonly described as the gentle giants of the ocean and reefs. Their tail is just that—a rudder with no barb. They also have the largest brain of all fish and are known to be intelligent and curious. Snorkelling with these large non-threatening sea creatures and observing their placid and graceful movements is such a joy.

But back to the problem of the parasitic hitchhikers. Unlike parrot fish, manta rays do not have beak-like mouths to prise off the ectoparasites. Nor do they have rough tongues to assist in their removal. It is also rare to see manta rays scrape themselves against sharp coral to aid removal. So, what do they do? They take themselves to a cleaning station in the same way we might take a mud-splashed car to a carwash for thorough cleaning.

The cleaning station is often a coral bommie or outcrop where numbers of cleaner fish congregate. The cleaner fish are usually small and fast-moving. One that is commonly seen on coral reef cleaning stations in the tropical waters of Australia, Asia and the Pacific is *Labroides dimidiatus*—the cleaner wrasse or blue streak, named for the electric blue stripe along its body. These nifty little fish have a pointed snout with teeth at the front of their jaw—the perfect tool for effectively picking parasites, dead skin and algae from various parts of the manta rays' extensive bodies.[93] Manta rays are said to retain a mental map of the best cleaning stations and will even wait in line to undergo an extended period of cleaning.[94]

And the outcome? The manta rays are relieved of their potentially threatening hangers-on and the cleaner wrasse have their hunger satisfied by a meal of mainly parasites. This is mutualism at work in the coral reef ecosystem—bringing relief and sustaining life by means of a most effective relationship.

Reflection 16:
What Do I Need?

Background

This photograph features two very small (3 to 4 millimetres in length) native Australian stingless bees (*Tetragonula carbonaria*). They are gathering pollen which is packed into yellow round balls on their hind legs to take back to their nest. In the process of collecting pollen, they play a critical role in plant pollination.

Insects, of which these tiny bees are but one type, are one of the most dominant forms of life on earth, being found in nearly every environment, from the extreme sub-zero temperatures in the Arctic to extreme heat conditions in deserts. It is believed that they are so successful due to a protective shell or exoskeleton, being small and able to blend in with their environment and having high reproductive rates. They also possess considerable genetic diversity and great potential for adaptation to different or changing environments.[95]

Insects consume plants, prey on other creatures, and decompose debris, carcasses and dung. Some can survive eating only poisonous plants and store the poisons for their own defence.[96] They are also an important source of food for other organisms. For example, it has been estimated that birds consume 400 to 500 million tons of insects globally each year.[97] At the same time, some insects can be a challenge for humans and domesticated animals because they destroy crops and carry vector diseases. On the balance, though, less than 1% of insect species are pests, and only a few hundred of these are consistently a problem.[98,99]

While, to many people, insects are merely an annoyance to be avoided or killed, they directly benefit us by producing honey, silk, wax and other products. Indirectly, they are critical as pollinators of crops and as natural enemies of pests and scavengers. Their place in earth's ecosystems is so significant that, without them, these ecosystems would collapse. Who would have thought that something so small could play such an important role in life on earth?

Reflection

Tiny native bees are fascinating: constantly in motion, flying purposefully from flower to flower, seemingly investigating and harvesting every skerrick of pollen, making room for each other to take their share and banding together, squadron-like, to try and help a hapless member pounced on by a flower spider—so much to note in such a small space. Just as we were fascinated observers of these tiny creatures, there is another who is also very aware of their being, but more than that, can claim ownership of them, along with all the other insects in existence and more:

*Listen, my people, and I will speak; I will testify against you, Israel: I am God, your God. … I have no need of a bull from your stall or of goats from your pens, for every animal of the forest is mine, and the cattle on a thousand hills. **I know** every bird in the mountains, and **the insects [including bees] in the fields are mine**. If I were hungry, I would not tell you, for the world is mine, and all that is in it.* (Psalm 50:7, 9-12)

The statements, constituting a broad sweep across creation—from the largest and wildest ('*every animal of the forest…are mine*') to the domesticated ('*the cattle on a thousand hills…are mine*'); from the least tamed ('*I know every bird in the mountains*') to the tiniest of all creatures ('*the insects in the field… are mine*')—emphasize that all creation belongs to God. These verses tell us God owns and knows ALL of his creation.

Why was the psalmist reminding his listeners of these truths? In the context of this psalm, the writer Asaph, a Levite priest, was particularly aware of a creeping irregularity in Israel's worship of God. A significant aspect of their worship was the different sacrifices they were to offer to God (Leviticus 1:1—7:21)—offerings to restore their relationship with him, express their thankfulness and reflect their obedience and trust. However, it seems that the Israelites had slipped into thinking that God needed the grain, the bread and the animal sacrifices they offered to him. The surrounding nations believed that their gods depended on offerings for their sustenance. Israel was slipping into similar thinking—that they were doing God a favour in religiously making their offerings.

To counter these dangerous misconceptions, in Psalm 50:9-12, the Israelites are reminded that God is completely different from these other gods. He, as the Creator of all that exists, doesn't need anything from his people. On the contrary, it is he who sustains the operations of the universe and daily cycle of the earth ('*The Mighty One, God, the Lord, speaks and summons the earth from the rising of the sun to where it sets*' [Psalm 50:1]). As such, there is no-one on whom nor anything on which he is dependent. Rather, it is he who gives life and provides all that is needed for life (Acts 17:25).

God needs nothing from us. However, he does require something of us: to act justly, show mercy and walk in humility before him. Recognizing our place in the created order as well as our privileged responsibility to serve is what is required of us and is to be outworked in relation to all God has created—our fellow human beings and the rest of creation.

Prayer

Father God, as Creator and Lord over all creation, help us to increasingly know and love you. Help us to act justly and be merciful towards people and this earth on which we and all your creatures live. Amen.

Reflection 17:
Seasons

Background

A new season is often heralded by the appearance of flowers. In the dry areas of Western Australia and South Australia, the large (up to 75 millimetres in diameter), striking flowers of this multi-trunked ooldea mallee (*Eucalyptus youngiana*) begin appearing in late winter and continue to do so through spring and into early summer. They are followed by the sturdy, ribbed gumnuts that are also a feature of this tree.

Seasons vary across the world. While the mid-latitudes have four seasons, the Arctic and Antarctic have two seasons (both cold but with different amounts of daylight), as do the tropics (both hot but with or without rainfall). Indigenous Australians have a further concept of seasons which is determined by their knowledge of changes in the environment signalling the availability of many different food resources.

What causes the seasons that we all experience, no matter where we live? Many believe the earth is hotter in summer because it is closer to the sun and that, conversely, in winter, it is further from the sun and hence cooler. This is incorrect because the earth is closest to the sun in winter.[100]

The earth has seasons because during its orbit around the sun it is tilted (23.5 degrees) on its axis, with its tilted axis always pointing to the same direction in space. This tilt causes seasonal variations in both the intensity of sunlight that impacts the earth's surface as well as the duration of daylight. The part leaning closer to the sun will have more light and heat (the warmer months) and the part leaning away from the sun will have less light and heat (the cooler months). Around 21 December, the Southern Hemisphere is angled towards the sun and receives the most direct radiation and energy.[101] Six months later (21 June), although the earth is now closer, it is angled away from the sun and hence receives less radiation and is cooler.

Reflection

There is a time for everything, and a season for every activity under the heavens: a time to be born and a time to die, a time to plant and a time to uproot, a time to kill and a time to heal, a time to tear down and a time to build, a time to weep and a time to laugh, a time to mourn and a time to dance, a time to scatter stones and a time to gather them, a time to embrace and a time to refrain from embracing, a time to search and a time to give up, a time to keep and a time to throw away, a time to tear and a time to mend, a time to be silent and a time to speak, a time to love and a time to hate, a time for war and a time for peace. (Ecclesiastes 3:1-8)

Of all the verses in the Bible's challenging book, Ecclesiastes, these are some of the most well-known, having formed the lyrics of Pete Seeger's folk song '*Turn! Turn! Turn!*'. For those who remember it, the tune made it easy to recall the lyrics. But what are they saying?

In his phrasing of opposites—'*to kill and heal*', '*to tear down and build up*', '*to search and give up*', '*to tear and mend*', '*to be silent and speak*', '*to love and hate*', '*war and peace*'—this ancient writer, identified as Qohelet, gives us a realistic picture of the spectrum of life events. He recognises that there is a rhythm to life—the seasons that occur between the bookends of our birth and our death (when we are 'planted' and 'uprooted'). In between these major events, life has its ups and downs, with one season rarely lasting a lifetime.

Verses 3-8 reflect the types of activities or responses that could be expected within the life span of those in Qohelet's era, most likely in an agricultural setting. Interestingly, however, most of these are familiar to us today, showing that the nature of life events has changed surprisingly little. Moreover, the beauty of the language used is that it can be read either literally or metaphorically. God can speak through these into our lives. '*A time to kill*' what? An unhealthy habit? A damaging relationship? Weeds in our life that might be choking our spiritual growth? Conversely, '*a time to heal*' what? A relationship? Ourselves? A block of degraded land? We might even add our own seasons—a time to raise children and a time to enjoy grandchildren, a time to care for others and a time to be cared for.

Just as we have no control over the seasons of the year, we may well have no control over these seasons in life which can catch us unawares and be brief or drawn out, difficult to bear or a joy and relief. Living them '*under heaven*' means that we accept each one as allowed by God. Whatever the season, we know that God is with us in it and can bring about his good purposes.

One thing that can span all the seasons is prayer: readily engaging in conversation with our Father in heaven, giving praise and thanks and seeking his wisdom, guidance, comfort and peace. In all our seasons—the joyful, the painful, the tiring, the unsettling or the more mundane—we have a Father in heaven who hears and answers prayer (Psalm 65:2).

Prayer

Father God, thank you for the varied 'seasons' in our lives. Thank you that you walk with us through all seasons, and that your purposes are always good regardless of which season we may be in. Amen.

Reflection 18:
Mighty Rock

Background

I (Bob) have long been fascinated by rocky mountains, and they are one of my favourite places to hike. The mountain opposite, Mount Yulludunida (1,225 metres), is one of several remnant volcanic rocky outcrops in the Mount Kaputar National Park, located in north-west New South Wales. This photograph was taken with a drone[102] to capture the length and dramatic nature of the mountain's structure.

While the Warrumbungle National Park is well known for its spectacular volcanic scenery, the lesser-known Mount Kaputar National Park to the east is well worth a visit for any who love spectacular mountain scenery, walking and photography. In its formation, two volcanos pushed the landscape up high above the surrounding plains. This was followed by erosion over a long period that has carved a dramatic landscape of narrow valleys, steep ridges and volcanic plugs. The park has several great examples of ancient trachyte cliff-edged lava terraces to walk on and explore, as well as a spectacular rock formation known as Sawn Rocks, the best example of 'organ-piping' in Australia.[103] The park is the traditional Country of the Gamilaroi people, for whom it provided a rich source of food, medicines and shelter. Reminders of their connection to this ancient landscape are evident in Aboriginal rock carvings, campsites, marks on trees and axe grinding grooves throughout the park.[104]

Mount Yulludunida may be mistakenly regarded as part of a volcanic crater; however, it is actually a ring dyke. These are formed when an underground pool of hot molten rock drains away. The pool's roof then collapses, forming cracks. Molten volcanic rock is then squeezed through the cracks to form dykes, which are roughly circular or partially circular in shape.

Reflection

Yes, my soul, find rest in God; my hope comes from him. Truly he is my rock and my salvation; he is my fortress, I will not be shaken. My salvation and my honour depend on God; he is my **mighty rock***, my refuge. Trust in him at all times, you people; pour out your hearts to him, for God is our refuge.* (Psalm 62:5-8)

Life is rarely a smooth ride from beginning to end. Most of us have experienced situations that really unsettle us—whether it be the destructive violence of a savage weather event, a prolonged drought, the unexpected diagnosis of an illness, challenging work conditions or a family blow-up. King David was going through a similarly difficult time. In his case, he was facing the attack of enemies at the instigation of his estranged son, Absalom, as well as opposition behind the scenes from some people who appeared to be with him, but who in fact, were not.

In verses prior to these, David decried the deliberate plotting and subterfuge of those seeking to have him replaced as king. In these verses, he talks to himself, reminding himself of truths as a means of encouragement and comfort. He does this by changing his focus—looking away from and beyond his situation (which does not mean forgetting about it or pretending it doesn't exist) and looking to God. In other words, he makes a conscious choice to go to God in the difficult circumstances and '*find rest*' in the One who has been his '*hope*' and '*refuge*'.

What does this 'rest' mean? It is not necessarily deliverance from the strife but rather a quiet place, a peace that comes from God in the middle of strife and turmoil and that is perhaps beyond understanding. These are verses for any of us in dire straits: '*with God all things are possible*' (Matthew 19:26) and '*God is the giver of hope*' (Romans 15:13). This is also the assurance David had—trusting not in others but in the loving faithfulness of God. In addition to '*finding rest*' and '*hope in God*', David intentionally uses the words '*rock*', '*fortress*', '*mighty rock*' and '*refuge*', likely drawing from his experience of these as reliably safe places in times of battle or siege. These words reflect David's experience of God as a solidly trustworthy protector. This underlies the encouragement he, as the king appointed by God, then speaks to his people—'*trust in him at all times, you people; pour out your hearts to him*'. God is big enough to handle all the cries of our hearts; he will hear them and can be relied upon to be there with us and respond.

We may not be battle-hardened or battle-weary warrior-tacticians, but we do understand the solid nature of rock, the protection that fortresses have offered throughout history and perhaps through experience, we understand the value and safety afforded by places of retreat or refuge. There are times when being able to withdraw to such a place is a true godsend and necessity. These verses of Psalm 62 do indeed speak as much to us today as they did to David and his people so long ago—'*Yes, my soul, find rest [quietness, stillness] in God*' … '*my mighty rock*' … '*for God is our refuge*'. May we know the reality of this in our lives, particularly in times of distress and challenge.

Prayer

Father God, thank you for the witness of those who have trusted you. Thank you that like a mighty rock, you are dependable, powerful and a place of rest in the midst of turmoil. Grant those of us in challenging circumstances the peace that comes from entering into this reality. Amen.

Reflection 19:
Refreshment

Background

While walking in nature, how memorable are those 'wow' moments! It might be a lovely flower, a small but incredibly detailed insect or a dramatic cloud formation before a storm. This snow-fed stream and waterfall on the Routeburn Track on the South Island of New Zealand was one of those for both of us. We couldn't but stop and enjoy the refreshment it gave our hearts and minds. During such moments, the emotions are hard to describe but may include awe, wonder and admiration.[105] Scientists are now finding evidence that being in nature has a profound impact on our brains, our well-being and our behaviour. It can help reduce anxiety, feelings of negativity and stress and also increase our attention capacity, creativity and our ability to connect with others.[106,107,108]

The powerful impact of nature is beautifully illustrated by author and disability rights advocate Helen Keller, who lost her sight and hearing at just 19 months of age. She said she always had the feeling that nature had the power to *renew* and *refresh* our minds, our bodies and our spirits. She wrote:

I am particularly fond of my early morning walk in the meadows near our home in Forest Hills, Long Island. Perhaps there is no thrill so great as that which comes with a walk in the freshness of morning air. Though I do not see, I can feel earth's eager awakening after a night of rest. I can feel the first gentle rays of the sun, smiling, 'Here we are again'. I can feel the yielding softness of dew-freshened soil. The keen sweet smells of nature-in-the-morning stream about me. And the acuteness of smell so noticeable in the blind is some compensation for their sightlessness. Now and then I pick a flower or a stalk of grass and examine it with my fingers. Each is a new revelation of the wonders of nature.[109]

Reflection

Times of refreshment are balm to the soul. When we came upon this lovely sight—clear water flowing over mossy rocks and forming aquamarine pools beside a wall of lichens, mosses and ferns in varying shades of green—we couldn't but be delighted. After filling our water bottles while drinking in the refreshing scene with its tapestry of colours, we felt noticeably invigorated—refreshment from God in a place ultimately the work of his ongoing creativity.

Refreshment may come from different sources. *The Lord is my shepherd, I lack nothing. He makes me lie down in green pastures, he leads me beside quiet waters, he refreshes my soul* (Psalm 23:1-3).

David, the shepherd boy who was anointed king of Israel, knew well what it was to lead his flocks in a dry and rocky landscape and find for them watering places surrounded by lush growth. He uses this imagery to speak of God's abundant provision and, with it, restoration: physically, mentally and spiritually.

In Psalm 19, another of David's psalms, he writes, '*the law of the Lord is perfect, refreshing the soul*' (Psalm 19:7). It is the word of God (at that time, the books of the law, but now we have the whole Bible) that is complete ('*perfect*'), lacking in nothing. Being guided by what's written in the Bible can lead us to turn away from wrong and turn or return to God's ways, which has a reviving effect on our life. Thoughtfully and humbly reading what God says through the Bible can give us insight into God, ourselves and life in general. It can help recalibrate our perspective, draw us into or strengthen our relationship with God and refresh us with faith, hope and love.

In the New Testament, the apostle Paul writes of being '*refreshed*' by the household of Onesiphorus (2 Timothy 1:16-17). Onesiphorus ministered to Paul in practical ways, perhaps with meals, which would have certainly refreshed Paul physically. '*May the Lord show mercy to the household of Onesiphorus because he often refreshed me and was not ashamed of my chains. On the contrary, when he was in Rome, he searched hard for me until he found me*' (2 Timothy 1:16-17). Furthermore, his presence and solidarity—a tangible sign of God's love and care—would have greatly encouraged Paul at a time when others had abandoned him.

On yet another occasion, Paul writes that the love of a '*fellow worker,*' Philemon, '*has given [him] great encouragement, because [Philemon had] refreshed the hearts of the Lord's people*' (Philemon 1:7). We are not told exactly what Philemon did, but Paul writes that he showed love '*for all [God's] holy people*' as an expression of '*his faith in the Lord Jesus*' and an act of '*partnership ... in the faith*'. Philemon's service in the name of Jesus and for the body of Christ clearly had the effect of revitalising those in the body.

Walking in nature, sitting and listening to the sound of falling water, drinking in a glorious sunrise, being gifted with meals or the fellowship of another in God's family, receiving other acts of kindness and generosity, reading the Bible and sensing God speaking through its words: all of these can bring us refreshment—release, renewal and restored vitality—readying us for the next steps in our lives.

Prayer

Lord, thank you for the times of refreshing you bring to our lives. May we be those through whom you bring refreshment to others. For those we know who are weary and worn out, we ask that they be refreshed and know your restoration. Amen.

Reflection 20:
Two Worlds

Background

Rock platforms, with their tidal pools and sea life can be fascinating places for adults and children alike. The darting movements of tiny fish or the waving tentacles of an anemone fixed to a rock wall, the slow-moving arms of a starfish or the quick scuttle of a crab into a dark crevice can reveal a whole new world that is so often invisible, immersed in the inflowing tide.

This photograph was taken in a 2-metre-deep rock pool south of Newcastle, New South Wales during an exceptionally low tide. The area under water is always so, whereas the exposed rocks are covered to varying degrees by the sea depending on the height of the tide and the size of the swell and waves. In contrast, the cliffs and hill in the background are always above water level. In a sense, we see two worlds (above and below water) separated by a transition zone. This zone is called the intertidal (or littoral) zone. It is an extreme ecosystem, as it is constantly subject to major changes, being exposed to the air at low tide and submerged in seawater at high tide. Furthermore, it is often impacted by massive seas, strong winds, extreme temperatures, changing salinity and dissolved oxygen, and the desiccating heat of the sun, along with predators, such as birds at low tide and fish at high tide.

The photograph serves to highlight the great differences between the world under the water and that above. The underwater world in this rockpool is a mass of cunjevoi and large brown algae, such as kelp and sea grapes, along with pink algae and green sea weeds. They drift back and forth with the incoming and outgoing flows and provide habitat for smaller creatures. It is vastly different to the more familiar environment in the world above with its coastal trees, shrubs, wildflowers, sandy soil and sandstone cliffs.

Reflection

Just as the photograph illustrates the reality of two 'worlds', so, too, does Jesus speak openly of two worlds or two kingdoms. Kingdoms were very much a part of Jesus's context and they are no less a foreign concept today—2,000 years later.

However, the two kingdoms of which Jesus speaks are the kingdom of God and that of this world. Jesus states that this world is governed by the prince (of this world), whose intentions are not good: he is quite satisfied to see the good in this world turned upside down and evil thrive. On the other hand, what is the kingdom of God like?

His much-respected teachings from the Mount (Matthew 5:1—7:27) are one place where Jesus expounds God's kingdom values. As one example, in many parts of the world, 'an eye for an eye' (originally intended as curbing and limiting revenge) is played out on an international and national level as well as in communities and families. However, Jesus says:

> 'Eye for eye, tooth for tooth.' Is that going to get us anywhere? Here's what I propose: 'Don't hit back at all.' If someone strikes you, stand there and take it. If someone drags you into court and sues for the shirt off your back, gift-wrap your best coat and make a present of it. And if someone takes unfair advantage of you, use the occasion to practice the servant life. No more tit-for-tat stuff. Live generously. (*The Message*, Matthew 5:38-42)

How much would putting this into practice change people's lives in this world?

Do God's kingdom values influence the kingdom values of this world? The values of God as revealed in the Bible have undoubtedly brought so much good to this world, for example, the abolition of slavery in Britain; the establishment of hospitals, clinics and schools in remote parts of the world; and the Street Side Medics in New South Wales, founded by recently honoured Dr Daniel Nour, whose Christian faith undergirds this medical service for the homeless. On the other hand, the desire to put biblical values into practice has often met opposition. In the late 1800s and early 1900s, a Christian Indigenous man, William Cooper, read the Bible and saw that it affirmed the dignity and equality of Aboriginal people, their right to be fairly treated and to own some of the land on which God had placed them. He fought for just political reforms for his people but to no avail. In 1938 he, together with other Aboriginal leaders, organised the first Day of Mourning on 26 January. This evolved into National Aborigines Day, which has now become NAIDOC week, during which the history, culture and achievements of Indigenous Australians are celebrated.[110] While he didn't live to see the changes he agitated for, William Cooper did mentor those who continued to successfully work for them. William Cooper's life experience was one where two worlds were in conflict, reflecting the reality that there is often opposition to the values of God's kingdom in this world.

Despite this, Jesus does not want his followers to escape from the pain and troubles of this world '*that [does] not know [God]*'. One of his final prayers before his death was, '*My prayer is not that you [God, the Father] take them [my followers] out of the world but that you protect them from the evil one … As you sent me into the world, I have sent them into the world*' (John 17:15-18).

For Further Reflection

How well does my life reflect the values of the kingdom of God?

Is God asking me to go to a particular people or part of this world and live out his values there?

Reflection 21:
Of So Much Value

Background

These two spectacular eastern curlews (*Numenius madagascariensis*) were photographed at Stockton Sandspit, Newcastle, a protected area for migratory shorebirds. As can be imagined, the distinctive long beaks of the eastern curlews are ideal for picking out crabs and molluscs from the sand or mud flats and for foraging for delicacies deeper in the mud.

Most migratory shorebirds observed in Australia follow the route that extends from the Arctic Circle, through northern Russia and Asia, across about 20 countries, and down to Australia. During March or April, they begin their northward migration, returning to breeding grounds on the Arctic tundra. They arrive in time to nest during the northern summer months, when they can take advantage of an abundance of insects before making the return journey to 'over-winter' at non-breeding grounds in Australia from July to October.[111] Australia is the destination for 75% of eastern curlews.

Migratory shorebirds, varying in size from only 20 grams to 900 grams, are amazing travellers, undertaking some of the longest wildlife migrations in the world. During the return migration, some species fly up to 25,000 kilometres and, over the course of their lifetime, may fly the equivalent of the distance from here to the moon (384,400 kilometres)! During the journey, they can lose up to 50% of their body weight; hence the importance of good food supplies. It is believed that these birds undertake the flight because of the abundance of food in the opposite hemispheres.

Unfortunately, however, analysis of 25 years of monitoring data from citizen science groups around Australia has shown that many unique migratory species are in rapid decline and closer to extinction than previously thought. For example, the eastern curlew has declined by 80%. The research has shown the main reason for this is the loss of habitat along the birds' migration routes,[112] with the biggest threat to their ongoing existence being the reclamation of tidal flats in eastern Asia.

Reflection

God is recorded as caring for two sparrows caught and sold for food. Would he be any less aware of the eastern curlews disappearing?

So do not be afraid of them [people], for there is nothing concealed that will not be disclosed or hidden that will not be made known. What I tell you in the dark, speak in the daylight; what is whispered in your ear, proclaim from the roofs. Do not be afraid of those who kill the body but cannot kill the soul. Rather, be afraid of the One who can destroy both soul and body in hell. Are not two sparrows sold for a penny? Yet not one of them will fall to the ground outside your Father's care. And even the very hairs of your head are all numbered. So don't be afraid; you are worth more than many sparrows. (Matthew 10:26-31)

The context in which these verses are spoken is important. Jesus is sending out his 12 disciples to engage in the work that he had been undertaking (Matthew 10:1-25). They are to go among their own people. They are to depend on God for enabling and can expect him to work through them. They will face antagonism, accusations and persecution. Just as it had not been easy going for Jesus, their teacher and Lord, so, too, would it not be easy going for them. Jesus does not play down the difficult nature of this ministry.

However, following his frank disclosure in Matthew 10:5-25, he now seeks to encourage them with four words recorded often in the Bible, including three times here—'do not be afraid'. These words are not only an acknowledgment that his disciples will know fear; they also open up a bigger picture. Jesus reveals whom they are not to be afraid of: people who can imprison, falsely accuse and physically hurt them. This is counterbalanced with whom they should rightly fear—God, who has power over more than the physical body, who has power over life after death. Jesus also tells them what they are to do in place of 'being afraid': continue to speak the truth that he has passed on to them. Finally, he tells them why they are not to be afraid. Having given them a mission to undertake, God is very aware of each of them and will look after them. To vividly illustrate the reality of this, Jesus again draws on nature. Sparrows are some of the smallest birds in the Middle East (and elsewhere) and were a very cheap source of protein. But Jesus has no doubt whatsoever that, despite their seeming insignificance, their little lives—from birth to death—are in God's care. Jesus explains that if this is the attitude of God (the unimaginably powerful author of all creation) towards such a tiny creature, how much more will he watch over and care for these sent ones who are *'worth more than many sparrows'*.

Fear can stop us from stepping out to where God wants us to go or into what he wants us to do and also from speaking out for him. We must ask ourselves if we truly believe that, regardless of what might happen, *'nothing can separate [us] from the love of God'* and that, as one whose name is written in heaven, each of us is precious to him.

Prayer

Lord Jesus, thank you that our Father God knows all that is going on and is there for all called according to his purposes. Encourage each one who is facing persecution for their faith and challenges in their ministry. May they draw strength from knowing how precious they are to you. Amen.

Reflection 22:

A Story of Trees

Background

This photograph of a snappy gum (*Eucalyptus leucophloia*) on the top of Dales Gorge in Karijini National Park, Western Australia, was converted to black and white to highlight the contrasting alive and dead branches. While the tree is well adapted to its rocky environment, some branches have died—perhaps the result of a bushfire or insect damage. A common reaction to a dead object or creature is to avoid it or remove it. This may well be because we tend to perceive dead things in the natural world as being undesirable or of little value. We fail to fully grasp their intrinsic importance.

Ecological studies have demonstrated that trees and branches that are dead are just as important to the forest ecosystem as healthy ones.[113,114,115] In fact, some trees support more wildlife when dead than when they are alive. Dead standing trees, living trees that are compromised by fungi or insects, and fallen branches or logs on the ground all provide habitat and food for animals. They provide hiding places and homes for numerous insects, birds, amphibians, mammals and reptiles along with hosting fungi, lichens and other organisms that are all crucial to the overall health of the forest.[116] It is now established that dead trees are so important that it is best that they are left in place when they fall.[117] In areas where management practices have removed dead or dying trees, forest ecosystems fail to thrive. Furthermore, branches, leaves or trees that fall on the ground can help moisture retention and, as they are finally broken down by fungi, bacteria and insects, provide crucial minerals to the soil to help new plants grow.

Not just in Australia but worldwide, halting forest degradation requires protecting and restoring key attributes of forest structure, including large deadwood structures such as tree hollows and logs. In addition, our understanding of the ecological importance of deadwood needs to be enhanced.

Reflection

The First Trees: Amongst the many trees in the garden of Eden, where two humans were placed, grew the tree of life and the tree of knowledge of good and evil. Eating from the former nourished life in all its goodness, whereas the forbidden act of eating from the latter had devastating consequences. Every aspect of the man's and woman's lives was affected—physically (pain and decay came into play), emotionally (shame and fear controlled them) and spiritually (wanting to avoid God their Creator, provider and companion, and inadequately addressing their newly perceived 'unclothedness'). All creation was affected, too. Decay and death contaminated the living world, and hostile elements emerged. Death brought life to an end:

No one can redeem the life of another or give to God a ransom for them—the ransom for a life is costly, no payment is ever enough—so that they should live on forever and not see decay. But God will redeem me from the realm of the dead; he will surely take me to himself. (Psalm 49:7-9, 15)

As the psalmist says '*the ransom for a life is costly, no payment is ever enough*'. We may pay for medical treatment or care that can save or prolong life for a time, but, eventually, we all die. However, the writer of this ancient poem-song is inspired with hope—'*God will redeem me from the realm of the dead*'.

A Dead Tree: Over 500 years later, God did pay 'the costly ransom'. He sent his son into the world '*not ... to be served, but to serve, and to give his life as a ransom for many*' (Matthew 20:28). How? Through a harrowing death on a cross made of wood. Although orchestrated by jealous, politically savvy men, Jesus's death happened within God's much higher plan—to graciously restore to humanity and the world a peaceful and life-giving relationship with himself:

Jesus of Nazareth was a man accredited by God to you by miracles, wonders and signs, which God did among you through him, as you yourselves know. This man was handed over to you by God's deliberate plan and foreknowledge; and you, with the help of wicked men, put him to death by nailing him to the cross. (Acts 2:22-23)

Nailed to the dead-wood of a once-living tree, Jesus Christ, the son of God, completed the undertaking to pay for the sins of the world (Hebrews 9:26). His death was necessary and willingly endured, but the story doesn't end there. Just like dead trees in a forest, the cross—used by the Romans to cruelly take life—in the wisdom, love and power of God becomes a means to life and hope.

The Tree of Life: '*But God raised him from the dead, freeing him from the agony of death, because it was impossible for death to keep its hold on him*' (Acts 2:24). In his resurrection from death by the power of God, Jesus showed that sin was paid for and death was defeated. Through his resurrection to life, he restored to the world the promise of eternal life— to know God closely and live eternally. The final book of the Bible, Revelation, presents a picture of life beyond the grave for those who follow Jesus. In their city home—the gloriously lit city of God —a particular tree grows—the tree of life. And the tree of the knowledge of good and evil? It receives no mention. Indeed, evil and death have been defeated by Jesus; it is life that flourishes.

Prayer

Worthy is the Lamb who was slain to receive power and wealth and wisdom and strength and honour and glory and praise! (Revelation 5:12)

Reflection 23:
Every Scar Tells a Story

Background

In the natural world, there are numerous examples of scarring. Hillsides may be scarred by landslides, forests may be scarred by bushfire, and animals maybe scarred through an encounter with a predator. This photograph, taken near Port Stephens in New South Wales, shows a partially submerged humpback whale (*Megaptera novaeangliae*) with numerous scars along its back and dorsal fin.

Usually, the first sign of a humpback whale's presence is the cloud of water vapour that shoots into the air from its two blowholes (just visible at the front of the whale) when it breaks the surface. The waterspout forms as the whale surfaces and exhales the bulk of the deoxygenated air in its lungs. The spout is largely made up of the warm air from its lungs condensing into water droplets as it mixes with the cooler ambient air.[118] In this instance, a colourful rainbow appeared in the waterspout, formed through the interplay between sunlight and the water droplets, adding to the beauty and wonder of what we were witnessing.

Over several weeks of whale watching, we noticed that some whales had visible marks on their skin, varying in size from a small round puncture to narrow lines over 60 centimetres. Research on whale scarring points to three main causes.[119] The first is human-induced threats, which include entanglement in fishing gear (seen in up to 50% of humpback whales) and ship strikes.[120,121] We actually saw and reported to ORRCA (Organisation for the Rescue and Research of Cetaceans) one whale that had a long rope caught around its tail and trailing behind. Second, attack by predators, including killer whales and cookie-cutter sharks, are evidenced in about one in five humpback whales, especially younger ones.[122,123] Third, and the most common reason for scarring, is the many extremely sharp barnacles attached to the skin against which a young calf or a mating whale may rub and be superficially wounded.

Reflection

Just as the whales' scars tell stories of their ocean life, so, too, does another set of scars tell a most significant story.

Thomas was one of the 12 disciples chosen to be with Jesus. However, following Jesus's death, John's gospel records that Thomas doubted the claim of his fellow disciples that they had seen Jesus alive—'We have seen the Lord!' (John 20:25). In response to them, he says, 'Unless I see the nail marks in his hands and put my finger where the nails were, and put my hand into his side, I will not believe' (John 20:25). Thomas was fully aware of how Jesus had died—a tortuous and shameful crucifixion under Roman rule, by which each hand of the outstretched arms was nailed to a cross-beam, and the feet to a wooden upright. We are also told that Jesus's side was pierced by a Roman soldier's sword to ensure he was dead. Knowing all this, Thomas had trouble believing that Jesus could possibly be alive. Sound familiar?

> A week later [Jesus's] disciples were in the house again, and Thomas was with them. Though the doors were locked, Jesus came and stood among them and said, 'Peace be with you!' Then he said to Thomas, 'Put your finger here; see my hands. Reach out your hand and put it into my side. Stop doubting and believe.' (John 20:26-27)

Jesus understood where Thomas was at—grieving, doubting and disheartened—and so encouraged him to see and feel for himself the scars on his resurrected body.

And the story told by those scars? They tell of one who had endured unimaginable torture through the most dishonourable of deaths generally reserved for criminals, slaves, and insurrectionists. Jesus was none of these, nor even a sinner: 'he who had no sin' (2 Corinthians 5:21). He had harmed no-one but, rather, taught truthfully and healed and ministered to many, regardless of status.

Jesus's sentencing and crucifixion were completely unjust. Yet, at no time during his trial or crucifixion did he resist or voice bitterness towards his accusers. Why? In submitting himself to such a humiliating death, Jesus was, in fact, submitting to a much greater plan—a divinely-initiated restoration plan—both cosmically profound and overwhelmingly gracious. Jesus's scars told a story of God's love for all his creation. They told of God's dealing with the reality of human sinfulness and evil in the world and of his justice in doing so. Moreover, the fact that Jesus could say to Thomas, 'Put your finger here; see my hands. Reach out your hand and put it into my side', meant that death did not and could not hold him. His body was scarred by it, but he was very much alive!

And Thomas's response after seeing for himself the scars on Jesus's body? 'My Lord and my God.' Thomas realised who stood before him. His joy, faith and hope were restored. And Jesus's response to Thomas? 'Because you have seen me, you have believed; blessed are those who have not seen and yet have believed' (John 20:29).

Every scar does tell a story. Jesus's scars tell of love, sacrifice and hope: the love of the God of the universe opening the way for us to live abundantly and in peace with him once again—in this life and in the life beyond death.

Prayer

Lord Jesus, full of grace, truth, and love, thank you for your deep compassion and Passion for this world. With the eyes of faith we see the scars that testify to your resurrection and we rejoice that in you is forgiveness and life. Amen.

Reflection 24:
Without Me

Background

This photograph of a climbing orchid (*Erythrorchis cassythoides*) on the trunk of a spotted gum (*Corymbia maculata*) was taken in a nearby open eucalyptus forest. The orchid is using the tree to support its 4-metre height, the upper one-third of which displays these beautiful, intricate yellow flowers. The orchid plant is leafless and, being non-photosynthetic, relies on root-dwelling fungi to provide a source of carbon for growth.[124]

This is a further example of commensalism, a type of symbiosis where there is a relationship between two organisms such that one benefits from the other without causing harm to it. The types of benefits may include food, support, transport or protection. Here, the orchid is supported by the tree to expose its flowers to pollinators. There are no documented benefits to the tree through this association with the orchid.

Another well-known example of commensalism that you may have observed is between cattle and cattle egrets, where the birds feed on insects flushed out of the grass by the grazing cattle. Generally, the birds increase their rate of feeding when following the cattle and, hence, clearly benefit from the association. A further example is the barnacles attached to humpback whales. The barnacles get a free ride (transport) into plankton-rich waters where the whales feed and they, too, can feed on the plankton without harming the whale.

Some other examples include sharks and remora, a type of sucker fish (transport, protection and food); milkweed and the monarch butterfly (protection from birds via the milkweed's toxin, which is harmless for the butterfly); and army ants and so-called antbirds (food—the birds follow the army ants and feed on insects fleeing from the ants. The birds benefit, and the ants are not harmed).[125]

Reflection

Reliance on another, exemplified by symbiosis in nature, is also a feature of human relationships, particularly for those called upon to be part of the kingdom of heaven:

> *I am the vine; you are the branches. If you remain in me and I in you, you will bear much fruit; apart from me you can do nothing. If you do not remain in me, you are like a branch that is thrown away and withers; such branches are picked up, thrown into the fire and burned. If you remain in me and my words remain in you, ask whatever you wish, and it will be done for you. This is to my Father's glory, that you bear much fruit, showing yourselves to be my disciples.* (John 15:5-8)

In an intimate conversation (John 14—17) with his disciples prior to his cruel death, Jesus seeks to reassure and comfort them as well as teach them some important truths to guide them in the coming times.

In the predominantly agricultural landscape of Judea, the grape vine was widely planted and cultivated for its seasonal bunches of fruit. Jesus draws on this to illustrate his teaching. Just as the climbing orchid depends on the tree for nourishment and support in producing and displaying its delicate flowers, and just as fruit-producing branches are nothing without a grape vine, Jesus states that his disciples need him and will continue to need him for *'apart from me you can do nothing'*. In preparing for his death, resurrection and leaving this world and his disciple-friends, Jesus appreciates they will *'still [be] in the world'*, continuing his work. He tells them this will be possible by *'remaining in him and he in them'* and that this close relationship will *'bear much fruit'*.

So how are they *'to remain in him'*? Just as vine branches reflect the genetic makeup of the vine out of which they grow and draw their nourishment, the disciples's lives are to be derived from him and formed by him as to their worldview, values, lifestyle, character, choices and actions. Likewise, Jesus will *'remain in'* them. How? In the same way that the vine continues to pour life into the dependent branches, the words of Jesus—his teachings—that his disciples have heard and pondered for the preceding 3 years are to continue shaping and guiding their inner being (enlightened by the Spirit of truth).

Similarly, if we are to be disciples of Jesus, bearing fruit for the kingdom of God, then we need to *'remain in him'* and let *'his words remain in us'*. When our inner life is lived in dependence on Jesus, producing fruit will be the inevitable outcome. What is more, in relation to this, Jesus makes an extraordinary promise—*'ask whatever you wish, and it will be done for you'*. Now it is clear that this *'wishing'* and *'asking'* will be determined by the effect of God's words remaining in us, but it promises the reality that *'whoever believes in me will do the works I have been doing, and they will do even greater things than these, because I am going to the Father'* (John 14:12). And the purpose of this? Not our glory, but that God is glorified in his kingdom coming. *'Then he went with them into the temple courts, walking and jumping, and praising God'* (Acts 3:8).

Prayer

Jesus, help me, I pray, to remain in you and I ask that you remain in me. Help me not to quench the Spirit but to live each day with an obedient heart and mind in both the little and the big things. Amen.

Reflection 25:
What Remains

Background

While camped at the Warrumbungle National Park in north-west New South Wales, we set off very early one morning (3.30am) with torches to walk to the Grand High Tops. Our aim was to capture the sun rising over this amazing volcanic landscape. The hike through eucalypt forest and up to the high tops in the dark brought new revelations of nature—the many tiny eyes of spiders reflecting brightly in the beam of our lights, the intermittent calls of owls and tawny frogmouths, the distinctive 'blonks' of Pobblebonk frogs along the creek and the awesome night sky, brilliant with stars and moonlight. On reaching the high tops in the pre-dawn light, we set up the camera. The best light for photography (lasting only minutes) was just before the sun broke the horizon when its warm cast intensified the orange-browns of the volcanic rock.

The main rock in the photograph is 'the Breadknife', so called because of its narrow, jagged shape. It is the most well-known and photographed formation in the national park. It is a dyke, formed during a high-intensity period of volcanic activity when hot magma (trachyte) flowed into a vertical crack in the surrounding rocks prior to hardening. In places, it is no more than a few metres wide, up to 60 metres high, and can be traced for almost a kilometre.[126]

Since the successive periods of volcanic activity, the surrounding softer volcanic rocks (pyroclastic breccia) that were formed from explosive fragmentation of lava, and other pre-existing rocks, have largely been eroded away.[127] This has exposed very hard, resistant volcanic remnants that were previously hidden, such as the Breadknife and nearby domes and plugs. The eroded material was deposited on valley floors and plains, producing rich, dark basaltic soils.

Reflection

As we sat in the early morning light and watched it transform the Breadknife and, in turn, other remnant outcrops into temporarily glowing rock formations, we were struck afresh by the powerful scenery. The landscape and character of the Warrumbungle National Park, so unique and distinctive, is dominated by the various formations that have remained from the volcanic activity and the subsequent erosive processes. Will these mighty rocks remain forever? No. In time, they, too, will fall or erode away and disappear into the landscape like the grasses that grow around their bases and in their cracks and crevices. Does anything remain?

All people are like grass, and all their faithfulness is like the flowers of the field. The grass withers and the flowers fall, because the breath of the Lord blows on them. Surely the people are grass. The grass withers and the flowers fall, but the word of our God endures forever. (Isaiah 40:6-8)

The fleeting nature of flowers and grass is what the prophet Isaiah drew on to depict the likewise transient nature of humanity. Regardless of a person's status, education or wealth, all lives are transient. To Israel, under the seemingly endless control of Babylon, it was a reminder that their oppressors would not live forever. To us, it speaks of the impermanence of our lives. What does remain?

Isaiah concludes with a dramatic contrast—*'but the word of our God endures forever'*. The contrast is striking—from humanity to God, from temporal to eternal, from creation brought into being by God's word and now bound by decay and death to the enduring and life-giving word, from transitory trustworthiness to enduring faithfulness. Isaiah is reminding the Jewish exiles that they have an extraordinary God—so far above and unlike humanity—on whom they can completely rely. In the same way, we, too, can trust what God says. His words are not said yesterday, gone today and meaningless into the future. They remain truthful and trustworthy forever.

The apostle Peter picks up these same verses in his first letter (1 Peter 1:23-25) to Christians in exile and uses them as an encouragement, especially to those facing persecution. He begins by reminding them that they *'have been born again, not of perishable seed, but of imperishable, through the living and enduring word of God'*. Their new life (re-birth) in Christ Jesus came from their hearing and responding to the *'living and enduring word of God'*. In turn, their new life, re-generated from God's word and his Spirit, will also endure. This work of the Holy Spirit through the word of God has moved them beyond a life that is physically reproduced and temporary, to a life that is eternal—already begun but only to be fully realised when *'the dead will be raised imperishable, and we will be changed … When the perishable has been clothed with the imperishable, and the mortal with immortality'* (1 Corinthians 15:51-54).

And this is not just for those Peter is addressing but for all of us who have experienced such a work of God in our lives. We are no longer defined by the temporary nature of existence in our current bodies. All followers of Jesus are ensured the reality of receiving an inheritance (1 Peter 1:3-4). That inheritance is life, eternal and abundant life in the kingdom of God—completely free, safe, at peace and in an uninterrupted, loving relationship with Jesus and God in a restored creation. This is what will remain.

Prayer

Lord Jesus, although our lives in this world are transient, thank you that the new life you have seeded and are growing in us will remain to your praise and glory in the kingdom of God and the Lamb. Amen.

Reflection 26:
What We Do to the Land Matters

Background

While photographing rural scenes in north-western New South Wales with a drone, a dust storm appeared, rapidly darkening the sky. Soon after landing the drone, we were engulfed by the dust, which reduced visibility to 100 metres.

Dust storms are the result of soil erosion by wind. The soil needs to be dry and exposed and, dependent on the size of the dust particles, the minimum wind speed 30 kilometres per hour. The main drivers are climate conditions (such as droughts), sediment supply and land management (overstocking, land clearing, mining).[128] Globally, it has been estimated that 25% of dust emissions have resulted from human activities such as agriculture and mining. In Australia, grazing by livestock along with feral animals have major impacts on ground cover and the physical properties of soil. Such impacts have been exacerbated with the establishment of watering points allowing animals (domestic and feral) to be active across previously dry parts of the continent. The effects of wind erosion include soil loss, reduction in soil nutrients and organic matter, reduced water infiltration and moisture-holding capacity and the exposure of unproductive subsoils.[129]

Dust storms also cause considerable economic and physical damage downwind as they deposit unwanted dust and reduce air quality, having a major impact on health.[130] In Australia, around 110 million tonnes of dust are transported annually.[131] While the impacts are predominantly negative, transport of eroded soil can provide nutrients to systems that can trap dust, such as forests.

Wind erosion appears to have been reduced substantially since the 1940s due to the better management of vegetation cover on agricultural lands, for example, by crop rotation, optimising stocking levels, increased tree planting and improved water management. However, it is expected that the incidence of huge dust storms will increase in the future because of climate change.[132]

Reflection

In recent times, a prolonged drought affected eastern Australia. It had devastating effects on crops, livestock, topsoil, water supplies and the livelihoods of many on the land. The land endured an enforced 'rest'. With subsequent good rains, it has rebounded with grasses, crops, trees and livestock flourishing.

The Lord said to Moses at Mount Sinai, 'Speak to the Israelites and say to them: "When you enter the land I am going to give you, the land itself must observe a sabbath to the Lord. For six years sow your fields, and for six years prune your vineyards and gather their crops. But in the seventh year the land is to have a year of sabbath rest, a sabbath to the Lord … "'. (Leviticus 25:1-4)

'"If … you still do not listen to me but continue to be hostile toward me … I will scatter you among the nations … Then the land will enjoy its sabbath years all the time that it lies desolate … then the land will rest and enjoy its sabbaths. All the time that it lies desolate, the land will have the rest it did not have during the sabbaths you lived in it …"'. (Leviticus 26:27, 33-35)

These verses in the book of Leviticus (written around 7th century BCE) reveal a concern of God's that may surprise us. The Israelites were about to enter their new homeland, where they would raise animals and grow vines and crops. In other words, they would depend heavily on the land. As such, and to ensure its ongoing fertility, God stipulates that the land be cared for. Moreover, he tells them how this can be done in a pre-industrial era. In addition to the weekly Sabbath of rest and worship, God instituted 7-year and 7-times-7-year sabbath cycles. The land was to be rested in every 7-year cycle.

How would this care for it? An agrarian society in that era did not have human-made fertilisers or such to promote crop and grassland fertility. They would have depended on the manure of their livestock and natural growth. This would have served them well for a time, but, to avoid over-use and irreparable depletion of soil nutrients, the land needed time to 'rest' and recover. That was to occur every seventh year.

In the subsequent verses, God is stating clearly what will happen if the Israelites break the covenant (their promised agreement) with him. If they choose to go their own way—living unwisely, unjustly and selfishly—they will lose the right to occupy the land. However, with their removal from it, the land would have the respite denied it in the many years Israel had not followed God's advice. The thrice-repeated, *'the land will have its sabbath rests'* (verses 33-35), speaks emphatically of God's concern for the land.

Stipulating that the land be rested every seventh year reflects God's understanding of how fundamental soil integrity was to productive farming. It also clearly reveals God's practical wisdom and care for his people. God looked beyond the short-term and prescribed a way of land management that would support longer-term productivity. This was to be part of a way of life that was about so much more than economic gain and immediate reward. Following this God-ordained rhythm of use and rest would, above all, reflect a trust in God that was to govern all of their way of life.

Prayer

Lord God, down through the ages, you have shared your wisdom and sought the best for all your creation as seen in your concern for the land. May your wisdom guide us not only in how we work and rest today but also in our use of and care for the resources you provide. May we trust you fully. Amen.

Reflection 27:
What is Truth?

Background

The intriguing day octopus (*Octopus cyanea*) is often not what it seems in its coral reef environment. As a daylight feeder, its ability to camouflage is amazing. Through nervous impulses sent from its complex brain to its muscles, it can rapidly change its appearance to resemble the sand, living or dead coral, or rock or mud on which it is resting. Over a 7-hour period, biologist Roger Hanlon observed one day octopus changing patterns 1,000 times![133] Its ability to do this makes it virtually invisible to predators. Is this an octopus or a piece of coral?

Most of the background sections in this book are based on science. Some may ask what is science, and what is the relationship between science, knowledge and truth? This is briefly set out in an article by the Australian Academy of Science:

Science can be thought of as both a body of knowledge (the things we have already discovered), and the process of acquiring new knowledge (through observation and experimentation—testing and hypothesising). Both knowledge and process are interdependent, since the knowledge acquired depends on the questions asked and the methods used to find the answers … While scientists may have a lot of data to support a theory, for example, that gravity does exist, they are constantly refining and reassessing the data. While certain theories are accepted as 'true', this is done provisionally. What is truth today, may be shown not to be so tomorrow … Science is … never finished. Every discovery leads to more questions, new mysteries, to something else that needs explaining. For example, the discovery of the double-helix structure of DNA revolutionised the understanding of biology and has brought up whole new areas to be studied such as genetic modification and synthetic biology.[134]

In a similar way, and in the spirit of Psalm 111:2 ('*Great are the works of the Lord; they are pondered by all who delight in them*'), new questions are being asked about the day octopus and, through those questions, further knowledge is being gained.

Reflection

Recently, the question uttered by the Roman governor during his interrogation of Jesus struck me afresh. Jesus had matter-of-factly stated, '*the reason I was born and came into the world is to testify to the truth. Everyone on the side of truth listens to me*' (John 18:37). Pilate, somewhat cynically, responded with, '*What is truth?*' (John 18:38)—a question as relevant today as it was then.

In the last few years, the term 'fake news' has become part of the vernacular. Fake news is a form of misinformation or disinformation. One consequence of its spread is that it may push us into certain ways of viewing the world without our questioning these views. Another consequence is that it can raise doubts about all news—is it all fake, or is it simply too difficult to know which is false and which isn't? This, in turn, can foster a state of apathy or reluctance to engage with matters that are important.

In some respects, this is what happened in Israel in the years 626 to 587 BCE when the prophet Jeremiah was called by God to speak to the people of that nation. Jeremiah was tasked with warning Israel of the perilous path down which they were travelling—rejecting both God, who had nurtured their growth into nationhood, and the radically different and just ways of living that he had prescribed. Instead, they had decided to follow the practices of the nations around them—'*their evil deeds have no limit; they do not seek justice. They do not promote the case of the fatherless; they do not defend the just cause of the poor*' (Jeremiah 5:28). However, the people and their leaders were fed 'fake news': '*A horrible and shocking thing has happened in the land: The prophets prophesy lies, the priests rule by their own authority, and my people love it this way*' (Jeremiah 5:30-31). Jeremiah's hard-to-hear message was countered by false messages—telling the people what they wanted to hear and making the prophesiers popular.

When Jesus was engaged in his 3 years of public ministry, many did not like what he was saying about God and his kingdom values. The latter included warnings to be alert to false prophets: '*ferocious wolves in sheep's clothing*'. This was a reference to the religious teachers who appeared harmless but, according to Jesus, were destroyers of a life-enhancing relationship with God (Matthew 5—7). Furthermore, some of the leaders and the people reacted strongly to the claims Jesus made about himself:

Thomas said to him, 'Lord, we don't know where you are going, so how can we know the way?' Jesus answered, 'I am the way and the truth and the life. No one comes to the Father except through me … If you really know me, you will know my Father as well. From now on, you do know him and have seen him.' (John 14:5-6)

Extraordinary claims? Were the religious leaders correct in thinking Jesus was crazy or an evil liar? Or was he speaking the truth? Those living in the time of Jesus had the opportunity to speak with him and see what he was doing in people's lives, and '*many believed*' (John 10:42). Truth from God remains that—truth. '*Jesus Christ is the same yesterday and today and forever*' (Hebrews 13:8). Truth may be hard to hear at times or not popular, but when we hold fast to Jesus who is truth, he continues to show us the way and give us life. This he has promised.

Prayer

Lord Jesus, may you and your words—the truth—increasingly mould and shape my being. May you as the way, the truth and the life be increasingly known, loved and followed in this world. Amen.

Reflection 28:
Being a Neighbour

Background

In the mainly tropical waters that flow between us and our neighbouring countries, sea turtles live. To come across one of these creatures while snorkelling is such a lovely experience—observing their gentle, unhurried yet purposeful movements in the underwater home that they share with so much other life.

According to the Smithsonian National Museum of Natural History, there are 7 species of sea turtles, all but one of which are listed as vulnerable to critically endangered on the IUCN Red List.[135]

The green sea turtle, in the photograph, begins life eating fish eggs, molluscs and crustaceans, but, after 3 to 5 years, it becomes a herbivore as an adult, eating only plant life, such as sea grasses, algae and seaweed. These turtles (if they are in the 10% that survive the hatchling stage) can grow quite large, up to 159 kilograms, with a carapace (top shell) of 1.4 metres. They live in a symbiotic relationship with certain fish that eat the algae from their shells. The fish gain food, while the turtles glide more freely through the water with their cleaner shells.[136]

The biggest threat to the green sea turtle's existence is human activity—intentional hunting; net fishing and the discarding of nets in the ocean, which can entangle turtles and prevent them from rising to the surface to breathe; and pollution, particularly from plastics that look like jellyfish, which are eaten by some turtles. Beach development and global warming are also interfering with nesting and the sex of the hatchlings.[137] Global warming is not only adversely affecting the lives of sea turtles but also the oceans and their related weather systems, thereby posing a threat to the many peoples who live in close proximity to the sea.

Reflection

In one of his interactions with listeners, Jesus was asked by an 'expert in the law', '*Who is my neighbour?*' (Luke 10:29) He asked this, as Luke comments, in order to justify himself. No doubt, he thought he was doing a pretty good job of 'loving his neighbour'. To answer his question, though, Jesus told a story of a Good (not lawyer, not priest, not innkeeper but) Samaritan (Luke 10:30-37)! This was a choice that would intentionally shock his listeners. Samaritans were a people whom the Jews in Galilee and Judah despised for worshipping other gods and whom they studiously avoided.

In addressing the question, '*Who is my neighbour?*', Jesus redirects the focus from limiting who a neighbour can be to emphasising what it is to be a neighbour: helping anyone we come across who is in need. What is more, as an example not easily forgotten, he presents the despised Samaritan as the model of love-in-action towards a stranger. And, as the story also illustrates, that love-in-action may entail a cost that should be willingly absorbed as part of the ministry of truly being a neighbour.

This story speaks deeply to how we should live on this earth. If we are followers of Jesus, then his teaching (the instructions, stories and parables) and his life (how he lived and what he did) give us clear but often hard-to-follow (in our own strength) guidelines. However, not only are we disciples, but we are also new creations with the presence of God—the Holy Spirit—in our being.

As such, God has given us new life and new power to choose to make his ways our ways, to fulfil our vocation in the kingdom of God—reconciling people to God and looking after his creation.

Jesus calls us to be people who do not ignore our neighbours but are considerate and proactive in helping them in their times of need. Is it really possible to say we care—to be the neighbours we are called to be—if, by our actions or those of the leaders we choose, we are contributing to the destruction of people's homelands and, thereby, their social and cultural structures, community and individual well-being? If our actions or—just as importantly—our inactions or decisions cause people to become, for example, climate change refugees, is that being a good neighbour? Taking positive action to help our neighbours might indeed cost us as a nation and therefore, individually. However, as Tim Costello wrote so pertinently in an article published in 2021, England faced a similar situation as it grappled with abolishing slavery—the unjust treatment of human beings for the benefit of others. But, through the persistent efforts of a group led by the Christian parliamentarian William Wilberforce, it did grapple with it! As a result, the slavery abolition bill was passed by parliament with a huge majority. Justice and righteousness prevailed, and England did not suffer for doing what was right under God.[138]

Prayer

Our Father in heaven, forgive us for all those times when we have not been a good neighbour. Help us, individually, as communities and as a nation, to love our neighbours as ourselves and to act justly towards them. We pray, too, that you would inspire our leaders to make decisions that promote life. Amen.

Reflection 29:
Abundance

Background

Each year about 36 species of migratory shorebirds fly 10,000 to 13,000 kilometres from breeding grounds in the Arctic, across East Asian countries, and arrive in Australia in late August to early September. Around 100,000 of these birds fly to Roebuck Bay on the Kimberley Coast in north-west Western Australia. Why?

Roebuck Bay is a sheltered marine environment subject to massive tidal changes. It comprises 34,119 hectares of mainly intertidal mudflats.[139] These mudflats have an abundance of benthic invertebrates such as tiny snails and top shells (up to 2,500 per square metre) making them a rich feeding ground for these vast numbers of birds. Because of its unique role in supporting these shorebirds, Roebuck Bay was National Heritage-listed in 2011 and designated a marine park and Indigenous Protected Area in 2016. It is the most significant migratory shorebird viewing site in Australia and one of the top four such sites in the world.[140]

The fully framed photograph of a number of these birds in flight understates their abundance but highlights an extraordinary aspect of their flight in a large flock. Despite their numbers and proximity to each other in the air, they do not collide. This is something that has puzzled observers for centuries. Researchers in Australia, using high speed video cameras, found that birds flying towards each other in a tunnel appeared to use two simple strategies for collision avoidance: each bird veers to its right, and each bird changes its altitude relative to the other bird for as yet unknown reasons.[141] For a flock flying in the same direction, sometimes at speeds over 50 kilometres per hour with rapid changes in direction and the birds separated by just over a body length, it is thought that individual birds pay close attention to just the few birds around them—their immediate neighbours[142]—but the research is still ongoing.

Reflection

The abundant and diverse shorebird life at Roebuck Bay is a sight to behold! There is something wonderful in observing so much life being provided for and sustained in a place that is safe and protected. In a sense, it speaks of a Creator who doesn't do things by halves:

> How many are your works, Lord! In wisdom you made them all; the earth is full of your creatures. (Psalm 104:24)

God creates extraordinary creatures in such diversity and abundance. He also generously and creatively sustains his creatures. The abundant life at Roebuck Bay also testifies to a diverse range of people working with him (consciously or otherwise) to nurture his creation. This includes local Indigenous custodians, volunteers, ecologists, teachers, students, researchers and government.

The abundant richness of creation reflects the glory of a Creator whose love also flows abundantly. John tells us not just that God loves, but that he IS love (1 John 4:8). This is hard to comprehend: the God of the universe, the living God is LOVE. Just as he has poured his love into making a world that was originally so 'very good', so, too, does his love flow towards people in so many different ways. This is echoed throughout scripture by writers whose illustrations give us insight into the nature of God's overflowing loving kindness.

In Psalm 103, David speaks of his experience of God 'who crowns [my soul] with love and compassion; who is compassionate and gracious, slow to anger, abounding in love and declares … as high as the heavens are above the earth, so great is his love for those who fear him' (Psalm 103:4, 8, 11). The generous yet tender love of God is captured by Isaiah in a beautiful shepherd image: 'He tends his flock like a shepherd: he gathers the lambs in his arms and carries them close to his heart; he gently leads those that have young' (Isaiah 40:11). The little ones, the vulnerable ones are 'carried close to God's heart', from where love flows.

In Isaiah 49:15, God's love is depicted as greater than that of a mother for the baby she has given birth to (he will never forget his children). This love for his people is further illustrated in Verse 16—'Behold, I have engraved you on the palms of my hands'—as though they are part of his very being and so precious to him. In the previous verses, God promised freedom and deliverance, but his people were despondent and believed that God had forgotten them. So what was his answer? Verses 15 and 16, with their beautiful pictures of his intimacy and love. How could he forget or ignore us and the challenges we face day-to-day when our name is written on his palm?

A similar theme of the abundance of God's love is found throughout the New Testament. For example, in his letter to the Romans, Paul writes that 'God's love has been poured out into our hearts through the Holy Spirit, who has been given to us' (Romans 5:5). God does not just trickle his love for us in little by little; rather, he pours it into us. There are times—drought-like times—when it is hard to feel God's love and even harder to show it, but that's when trust, based on verses such as the above, can be exercised and our recall of our experiences of God's love and care can inspire us. And perhaps even the image of abundant birdlife can remind us that God the generous Creator is also our heavenly Father who enfolds us in his love that is outworked in kindness.

Prayer

Now to him who is able to do far more abundantly than all that we ask or think, according to the power at work within us, to him be glory in the church and in Christ Jesus throughout all generations, forever and ever. Amen. (Ephesians 3:20)

Reflection 30:
Grief

Background

Taken at the top of a high mountain west of Alice Springs, this photograph shows the central rock-rat (*Zyzomys pedunculatus*). It was believed to be extinct until the rediscovery of several small populations in 1996. Historically, the species occurred across a wide area of Central Australia. Unfortunately, it is now restricted to just a few high mountain refuges and classified as 'critically endangered', with predation by feral cats being a major threat.[143]

Since European colonisation, the Australian land mammal population has suffered the highest rates of extinction of any mammal species worldwide. In 2019, 134 species or subspecies of mammals were at risk of extinction and listed as 'threatened' under the Environment Protection and Biodiversity Conservation Act 1999. Of these, 10 were critically endangered, with at least 7 predicted to be extinct within 20 years.[144] Feral cats are not just a key threat to the survival of the central rock-rat; they have been strongly implicated in the decline and extinction of many Australian mammal species.

Improved scientific knowledge, along with increased awareness and support by government and nature conservation groups, has led to some innovative approaches to stop population declines and extinctions. For example, for the central rock-rat, the Northern Territory Department of Environment, Parks and Water Security has adopted a 10-year recovery plan. This will include reducing the impacts of feral cats and determining and applying favourable fire management practices.[145] Other approaches being trialled include the expansion of national parks and conservation areas, relocation of threatened mammal species, breeding programs, feral-cat baiting and fencing off large areas for refuge and protection from predators.

Across the world, ecologists and other scientists are seriously concerned about the rate of disappearance of not only plant and animal life but also ecosystems that support them. For some, it is a source of frustration and even grief.

Reflection

It is not only people who grieve. Have you ever thought about God grieving? Both the Old and New Testaments tell us he does. What causes his grief?

In the Old Testament, Isaiah the prophet is recorded as saying:

> He [God] said, 'Surely they are my people, children who will be true to me'; and so he became their Saviour. In all their distress he too was distressed, and the angel of his presence saved them. In his love and mercy he redeemed them; he lifted them up and carried them all the days of old. Yet they rebelled **and grieved his Holy Spirit**. (Isaiah 63:8-10)

The people of Israel were to be integral to God's rescue plan for the world. As people chosen by him, they were to live in such a way as to be a living example of what God's way for this earth and its peoples looked like. By so doing, they would be like a beacon, drawing other nations into a living relationship with their Creator. However, Israel chose to rebel and be like their peers in the surrounding nations. This was a much easier choice but one that grieved the God who had cared for them, guided them and loved them deeply. As Isaiah states, they 'grieved his Holy Spirit'. In lamenting their rejection of him and his ways and what would happen to them, God also says in Jeremiah, 'I will weep and wail for the mountains and take up a lament concerning the wilderness grasslands. They are desolate and untraveled, and the lowing of cattle is not heard. The birds have all fled and the animals are gone' (Jeremiah 9:10). Israel's alienation from God is reflected in creation, and this causes God to grieve further. Nevertheless, God did not abandon them or his rescue plan for humanity.

Hundreds of years later, 'the Word [God] became flesh and made his dwelling among us'. Jesus (the Word)—'full of grace and truth' (John 1:14)— revealed God and fulfilled his role in the great rescue. Jesus never grieved God, rather, he was the son with whom God was 'well-pleased', but he certainly grieved over the condition of humankind and his people's hard-heartedness. Jerusalem brought him to tears. 'If you, even you, had only known on this day what would bring you peace—but now it is hidden from your eyes' (Luke 19:41-42). Like his Father, Jesus lamented that the people of Jerusalem, particularly its leaders, had rejected his message of reconciliation. The death of his friend Lazarus also brought Jesus to tears. He wept prior to raising Lazarus to life in a world still bound in death and decay. Perhaps this and the heartache and loss caused by his death were what so grieved Jesus. Only with his resurrection from his own death would death be overcome.

What of us? Having become God's children, gifted with the Holy Spirit, can we grieve our Father in heaven? Most certainly! In his letter to the church at Ephesus, Paul writes 'do not grieve the Holy Spirit of God, with whom you were sealed for the day of redemption' (Ephesians 4:30). This verse sits between others that give insight into how we might grieve the Holy Spirit. Paul writes of dishonest speech and actions, malicious talk, self-centred attitudes and emotions, sexual immorality, unholiness and greed. All these can contribute to spoiling relationships and damaging the environment in which we live.

Would any of us want to be known as people who cause intentional grief to our Father in heaven?

Prayer

Father, forgive us for all the times we have grieved you through our thoughts, words and actions towards you, others and this earth that is yours. Create in us a clean heart and renew a right spirit in us. Amen.

Reflection 31:
A Tale of Hope

Background

We have spent many wonderful hours sitting on a rocky headland photographing humpback whales (*Megaptera novaeangliae*) on their migration from the Antarctic to north-eastern Australia. At this location, over 170 humpback whales were counted on one day as part of the 2021 Whale Migration Census. Our vantage point was popular with many other enthusiastic whale-watchers, keen to observe these enormous creatures, up to 16 metres in length and 50 tonnes in weight.

Shortly after European colonisation, whaling and the export of whale products became Australia's first primary industry. The development of harpoon guns, explosive harpoons and motorised whaling boats made large-scale commercial whaling so efficient that, in the 20th century, many whale species were over-exploited and came very close to extinction. By the time the International Whaling Commission banned humpback whaling in the Southern Hemisphere in 1963, the population had declined to an estimated 3.5% to 5.0% of pre-whaling abundance, leading to the collapse of Australia's east coast whaling industry.[146]

Since the killing of humpback whales ceased, there has been a remarkable recovery in the numbers migrating annually along Australia's coastline from their feeding grounds in Antarctica to warmer waters for breeding. This is one of the more dramatic international marine life recoveries, with an estimated growth from 1,400 to 40,000 for the Australian populations.

Most Australians now consider the humpback whales to be of more value alive (both environmentally and economically), when, not so long ago, only dead whales were valued—as a source of oil, meat and baleen ('whalebone')![147] While this is to be celebrated, monitoring needs to continue due to new and ongoing threats including underwater noise interference, pollution, entanglement, overharvesting of prey, habitat degradation, and climate change.[148]

Reflection

*Praise the Lord from the earth, **you great sea creatures** and all ocean depths, lightning and hail, snow and clouds, stormy winds that do his bidding, you mountains and all hills, fruit trees and all cedars, wild animals and all cattle, small creatures and flying birds, kings of the earth and all nations, you princes and all rulers on earth, young men and women, old men and children. Let them praise the name of the Lord, for his name alone is exalted; his splendour is above the earth and the heavens.* (Psalm 148:7-13)

This psalm calls us to wholeheartedly acknowledge God as uniquely Lord over all that has been brought into existence and is sustained in an ordered system on the one and only blue planet. The first verses of this psalm call on all that are in the heavens—both animate (angels and heavenly hosts) and inanimate (sun, moon and stars)—to praise God. In the next verses, the earth and all that dwell in it—both animals and people as created beings—are also called to pour forth praise.

Normally, in the psalms and other passages in the Bible, the sea and some sea creatures are associated with uncontrollable forces (from a human perspective) and even chaos. However, the inclusion of the '*great sea creatures and all the ocean depths*' in this exhortation to praise God highlights that they, like all other creatures, live under one so much greater—their Creator and Lord.

Have we thought of creatures as praising God? Or have we only thought of humans as capable of praising God? Creatures have voices and bodies, and, while we may not know how they praise God, the psalmist takes it for granted that they

do so. Perhaps it is easy to imagine early morning birdsong as praise to God; but what of '*the great sea creatures*'? Of all the various '*great sea creatures*', those that readily come to mind are the whales. In thinking of these creatures praising God, we might well wonder if it is their joyful leaping and powerful breaching that are acts of praise or their repeated tail and fin-flapping? Is it the noises they make as they plough through the vast distances of ocean or the singing as they congregate in safe waters? Or is it simply by fully being whales that they praise God?

How wonderful it is to see the '*great sea creatures*'—in particular, the whales that were once so close to extinction at the hands of a fellow-creature, humankind—now free to live out their lives in the oceans of the world and, in so doing, join in the chorus of praise to their Lord and Creator. Understanding that, regardless of whether we are '*kings of the earth and all nations, princes and rulers on earth, young men and women, old men and children*', we, too, are creatures, has profound implications. As created beings, we are in it together with all the other creatures when it comes to praising God. It acknowledges that God is the One whose '*name alone is exalted*'. Our task is to live as his representatives in looking after the world, to let his values be our values, his care be our care and to live as part of '*creation's choir in heaven and earth, which has never ceased its praise*'.[149]

Prayer

Praise God from whom all blessings flow; praise Him all creatures here below; praise Him above, you heavenly host. Praise Father, Son and Holy Ghost. Amen.

Reflection 32:
God Does Care

Background

To see a small bird like the eastern spinebill (*Acanthorhynchus tenuirostris*) going about its daily life, oblivious of human presence, is such a delight! Using its long, downcurved bill, it probes deep into flowers like this grevillea to feed on the sweet nectar.

The current status of our global natural environment has been well documented in two recent comprehensive international reports.[150,151] The chair of the Intergovernmental Science-Policy Platform on Biodiversity and Ecosystem Services (IPBES), Sir Robert Watson, in releasing their report, said:

The health of ecosystems on which we and all other species depend is deteriorating more rapidly than ever … The diversity within species, between species and of ecosystems, as well as many fundamental contributions we derive from nature, are declining fast.[152]

In a comprehensive State of the World's Forests report[153], it is highlighted that despite some improvements, deforestation and forest degradation continue to take place at alarming rates (10 million hectares per year from 2015 to 2020). The majority of terrestrial biodiversity is found in the world's forests, which contain more than 60,000 different tree species and provide habitats for 80% of amphibian species, 75% of bird species and 68% of mammal species. About 60% of all vascular plants are also found in tropical forests.

Recognising the broad impacts of deteriorating ecosystems, including forests, Sir Robert Watson went on to say at the launch of the IPBES report, '*We are eroding the very foundations of our economies, livelihoods, food security, health and quality of life worldwide*'.[154] The essential, interconnected web of life on earth, of which we are a part, is getting critically disrupted, smaller and more fragile. However, importantly, the report also tells us that it is not too late to make a transformative difference—we have the means, but only if we start now, at every level from local to global.[155]

Reflection

Last year, while walking through a nearby forest reserve, it was impossible not to notice how alive it was with birdlife in the warmer-than-usual early morning air. The sweet melody of the golden whistler, the bell-like sounds of crimson rosellas, the high-pitched piping of an eastern spinebill and the busy squawking of rainbow lorikeets rung out from the tree-tops. Suddenly, two dear little grey fantails flitted into view. They perched in a nearby bush, repeatedly opening their delicate fan-like tails before flying off again.

The words from Psalm 36 came to mind:

*Your love, Lord, reaches to the heavens, your faithfulness to the skies. Your righteousness is like the highest mountains, your justice like the great deep. You, Lord, preserve both **people and animals**. How priceless is your unfailing love, O God!* (Psalm 36:5-7)

Out of his never-ending love God '*preserves both people and animals*'. This coupling of '*people*' [us] and '*animals*' is significant. Why? Because it tells us that God cares for all of his creation. He does so generously and unstintingly. As people made in the image of God, do we reflect his generosity towards his whole creation, including creatures? It is easy to be delighted by them (and God assuredly enjoys our delight), but do we live generously in relation to them?

In preserving people and animals, God provides what is needed for life. The birds that were heard and seen on the morning walk are provided for. In their forest home, they have trees or hollows in which to build nests. Flowering plants and the insects that feed on them provide their food. Streams and ponds together with dew and rainfall supply them with water.

This forest home grew out of one man's vision to rehabilitate a former coalmine. Since then, this forest has survived several threats to its existence because, over the years, people have protected it and the life in it. When it was threatened, they spoke out and acted. To have not done so would have been the equivalent of letting this forest in the city and all the life it supports be destroyed.

Caring for nature—the remarkable work of God—should be front and centre of our thinking as followers of Jesus. Why? Because it fulfils the very first delegated responsibility God gave humankind, who were made in his likeness to act as he would (Genesis 1:26-28). Included in that mandate was the freedom to wisely and creatively manage the extraordinary gifts in creation that God has given us. This has never been a permit to abuse or exploit creation to its detriment and to the detriment of people and future generations. That is not how God would treat his creation. He cares for it all—people, animals, air, soil, water, plants, habitats and ecosystems. As people called by Christ to be his body—the church—we should be leading the way in caring for creation that has been '*created through him and for him*' (Colossians 1:16). Delighting in creation, caring for creation and wisely using the resources gifted to us need to be recognised as important aspects of our worship of the living God, '*the Maker of heaven and earth, the sea, and everything in them*' (Psalm 146.6).

Meditation

I have walked, deliberately, often falteringly, towards a lifestyle in which I am trying to honour all that God has made. Does that mean I always get it right, or that there is nothing else I can learn, or do? Definitely not. But I believe that doing something is always better than doing nothing, which is why the motto that I have adopted over the years is: 'Many little steps in the right direction'—Ruth Valerio, Global Advocacy and Influencing Director, Tearfund.[156]

[Jesus] is the image of the invisible God, the firstborn of every creature: For by him were all things created, that are in heaven, and that are in earth, visible and invisible, whether they be thrones, or dominions, or principalities, or powers: all things were created through him, and for him.

(Colossians 1:15-16)

I lift up my eyes to the mountains—

where does my help come from?

My help comes from the Lord,

the Maker of heaven and earth.

(Psalm 121:1-2)

Who has measured the waters in the hollow of his hand,

or with the breadth of his hand marked off the heavens?

Who has held the dust of the earth in a basket,

or weighed the mountains on the scales

and the hills in a balance?

Who can fathom the Spirit of the Lord,

or instruct the Lord as his counselor?

(Isaiah 40:12-13)

In his hand are the depths of the earth,

and the mountain peaks belong to him.

The sea is his, for he made it,

and his hands formed the dry land.

(Psalm 95:4-5)

References

1 Stuart-Smith, S. (2020). *The well gardened mind.* William Collins.

2 Packer, J.I. (2013). *Knowing God.* Hodder & Stoughton.

3 Berry, R.J. & Meitzner Yoder, L.S. (2021). *John Stott on creation care.* IVP Books.

4 Pook, E., Gill, A. & Moore, P. (1997). Long-term variation of litter fall, canopy leaf area and flowering in a *Eucalyptus maculata* forest on the south coast of New South Wales. *Australian Journal of Botany, 45,* 737–755.

5 Higgins, L. (n.d.). *Take a moment to listen the trees. Trees don't have heartbeats.* Natural History Museum. https://nhm.org/stories/take-moment-listen-trees

6 Trees for the Future. (n.d.). *How to calculate the amount of CO2 sequestered in a tree per year.* https://www.unm.edu/~jbrink/365/Documents/Calculating_tree_carbon.pdf

7 Keith, H., Mackey, B. & Lindenmayer, D. (2009). Re-evaluation of forest biomass carbon stocks and lessons from the world's most carbon-dense forests. *Proceedings of the National Academy of Sciences, 106*(28) 11635-11640; DOI: 10.1073/pnas.0901970106

8 Stancil, J. (2019, 3 June). *The power of one tree - the very air we breathe.* US Department of Agriculture. https://www.usda.gov/media/blog/2015/03/17/power-one-tree-very-air-we-breathe

9 City of Newcastle and Awabakal Aboriginal Land Council's signage at Kau Ma Park. Burraghihnbihng and Hexham Swamp are registered dual names for this location.

10 Australians Together. (2021, 1 July). *The importance of land.* https://australianstogether.org.au/discover/indigenous-culture/the-importance-of-land/

11 Deadly Story. (n.d.). *Food and agriculture.* https://www.deadlystory.com/page/culture/Life_Lore/Food

12 Weir, J., Stacey, C., Youngetob, K. (2011). *The benefits associated with caring for Country.* Australian Institute of Aboriginal and Torres Strait Islander Studies. https://aiatsis.gov.au/sites/default/files/research_pub/benefits-cfc_0_2.pdf

13 Ward, A. (2021, 10 March). *'Country, land, knowledge': Aboriginal culture informing environmental water deliveries and restoring native water systems.* ABC News. https://www.abc.net.au/news/2021-03-10/chowilla-channels-ancient-culture-for-environmental-water/13226838

14 Mosco, R. (2017, 12 April). *A beginner's guide to common bird sounds and what they mean.* Audubon. https://www.audubon.org/news/a-beginners-guide-common-bird-sounds-and-what-they-mean

15 Birdlife Australia. (n.d.). *Superb lyrebird.* https://www.birdlife.org.au/bird-profile/superb-lyrebird

16 Ackerman, J. (2020). *The bird way: A new look at how birds talk, work, play, parent, and think.* Scribe.

17 Audubon. (2018, 16 July). *A wave of bird alarm calls can travel at 100 miles per hour.* https://www.audubon.org/news/a-wave-bird-alarm-calls-can-travel-100-miles-hour

18 Bible Project. (n.d.). *Shema / Listen* [Video]. https://bibleproject.com/explore/video/shema-listen/

19 Dear, J. & Butigan, K. (2016). An overview of Gospel nonviolence in the Christian tradition. In *Nonviolence and just peace: 11–13 April 2016, Rome, Italy. Background papers* (pp. 31–38). https://nonviolencejustpeacedotnet.files.wordpress.com/2016/05/nvjp-conference-background-papers.pdf

20 Atlas of Living Australia. (n.d.). *Helmeted gecko.* https://bie.ala.org.au/species/urn:lsid:biodiversity.org.au:afd.taxon:11871507-23a2-4aed-ad8d-c2c76d472f79

21 Backyard Buddies. (n.d.). *Geckos.* https://backyardbuddies.org.au/backyard-buddies/gecko/

22 Roberts, T. (n.d.). *Discovering geckos' sticky secrets.* University of Idaho Department of Biological Sciences. https://www.uidaho.edu/sci/biology/news/features/2014/geckos-sticky-feet

23 Murphy, M., Murphy, J., Faris, C. & Mulholland, M. (2019). Marooned on an extinct volcano: The conservation status of four endemic land snails (Gastropoda: Pulmonata) at Mount Kaputar, New South Wales. *Proceedings of the Linnean Society of New South Wales, 141,* S33–S44. https://openjournals.library.sydney.edu.au/index.php/LIN/article/view/14130

24 Jobling, A. (2013, 15 July). *Australia – Land of the hot pink slug.* Biodiversity Revolution. https://biodiversityrevolution.wordpress.com/2013/07/15/australia-land-of-the-hot-pink-slug/

25 ABC News. (2020, 29 January). *Park rangers feared the iconic neon pink Mount Kaputar slugs were wiped out by bushfires — then it rained.* https://www.abc.net.au/news/2020-01-29/giant-pink-slug-mount-kaputar-national-park-survived-bushfire/11911308

26 Murphy, M. & Shea, M. (2014). Survey of the land snail fauna (Gastropoda: Pulmonata) of Mount Kaputar National Park in northern inland New South Wales, Australia, including a description of the listing of Australia's first legally recognised endangered land snail community. *Molluscan Research, 35,* 51–64. https://doi.org/10.1080/13235818.2014.948147.

27 Houghton, J. T. (2013). *In the eye of the storm.* Lion Books.

28 A Rocha International. (2013). *John Stott London lecture 2013: Creation care – Revd Dr Chris Wright* [Video]. YouTube. https://www.youtube.com/watch?v=wvsqrFizQ7k

29 Ibid

30 National Aeronautics and Space Administration. (2015, December). *The Milky Way Galaxy*. https://imagine.gsfc.nasa.gov/science/objects/milkyway1.html

31 The Nine Planets. (2021, 4 January). *The Milky Way facts*. https://nineplanets.org/milky-way/

32 National Aeronautics and Space Administration. (2015, December). *The Milky Way Galaxy*. https://imagine.gsfc.nasa.gov/science/objects/milkyway1.html

33 National Aeronautics and Space Administration. (2017, 7 August). *Supermassive black hole Sagittarius A**. https://www.nasa.gov/mission_pages/chandra/multimedia/black-hole-SagittariusA.html

34 Couture, E. (2015, 18 September). *Ten facts about the Milky Way*. Versant Power Astronomy Center, University of Maine. https://astro.umaine.edu/10-facts-about-the-milky-way/

35 The Planets. (n.d.). *Milky Way*. https://theplanets.org/milky-way/

36 National Aeronautics and Space Administration. (2016, 14 October). *Hubble reveals observable universe contains 10 times more galaxies than previously thought*. https://www.nasa.gov/feature/goddard/2016/hubble-reveals-observable-universe-contains-10-times-more-galaxies-than-previously-thought

37 Guzik, D. (2020). *Psalm 19 – The heavens, the word, and the glory of God*. Enduring Word. https://enduringword.com/bible-commentary/psalm-19/

38 Land for Wildlife – South East Queensland. (n.d.). *Stinging trees: plants that make you go hmmm…* https://www.lfwseq.org.au/stinging-trees-plants-that-make-you-go-hmmm/

39 Dowling, A. (n.d.). *24 creatures that have lifespans worth talking about*. Animalogic. https://animalogic.ca/blog/24-creatures-that-have-lifespans-worth-talking-about

40 Roser, M. (2018, 8 October). *Twice as long – Life expectancy around the world*. Our World in Data. https://ourworldindata.org/life-expectancy-globally

41 United Nations. (2019, 17 June). *World population prospects 2019: Highlights*. United Nations Department of Economic and Social Affairs. https://www.un.org/development/desa/publications/world-population-prospects-2019-highlights.html

42 ABC Iview (2022, 7 April). *Miriam's deathly adventure. Episode 2*. https://iview.abc.net.au/show/miriam-s-deathly-adventure

43 Crockett, C. (2019, 7 September). *What is the electromagnetic spectrum?* EarthSky. https://earthsky.org/space/what-is-the-electromagnetic-spectrum/

44 Photon Terrace. (n.d.). *The basic nature of light*. https://photonterrace.net/en/photon/behavior/

45 National Oceanic and Atmospheric Administration. (2019, 1 February). *Aquatic food webs*. https://www.noaa.gov/education/resource-collections/marine-life/aquatic-food-webs

46 Commonwealth Scientific and Industrial Research Organisation. (n.d.). *Protecting native orchids*. https://www.csiro.au/en/research/plants/native/protecting-native-orchids

47 Brewer, G. (2020, 27 January). *Sneaky orchids and their pollination tricks*. Kew Royal Botanic Gardens. https://www.kew.org/read-and-watch/orchid-pollination-tricks

48 National Oceanic and Atmospheric Administration. (2021, 26 February). *How much oxygen comes from the ocean?* National Ocean Service. https://oceanservice.noaa.gov/facts/ocean-oxygen.html

49 Ocean Conservation Trust. (n.d.). *Why is the ocean important?* https://oceanconservationtrust.org/think-ocean/why-is-the-ocean-important/

50 United Nations Environment Program. (n.d.). *Why do oceans and seas matter?* https://www.unep.org/explore-topics/oceans-seas/why-do-oceans-and-seas-matter

51 Duerr, A. (2019, 9 April). *Fly like an eagle? Topography tells us how high Golden Eagles soar*. American Ornithological Society. https://americanornithology.org/fly-like-an-eagle/

52 Journey North. (n.d.) *How eagles fly*. https://journeynorth.org/tm/eagle/EagleFlightLesson.html

53 Duerr, A. (2019, 9 April). *Fly like an eagle? Topography tells us how high Golden Eagles soar*. American Ornithological Society. https://americanornithology.org/fly-like-an-eagle/

54 Rabiano, M. (2020, 4 September). *These masters of the sky can fly for hours (or days) while barely flapping*. Audubon. https://www.audubon.org/news/these-masters-sky-can-fly-hours-or-days-while-barely-flapping

55 New South Wales National Parks & Wildlife Service. (2010). *Glenrock State Conservation Area plan of management*. https://www.environment.nsw.gov.au/-/media/OEH/Corporate-Site/Documents/Parks-reserves-and-protected-areas/Parks-plans-of-management/glenrock-state-conservation-area-plan-of-management-100835.pdf

56 Joni Mitchell. (2021, 18 February). In *Wikiquote*. https://en.wikiquote.org/w/index.php?title=Joni_Mitchell&oldid=2928481

57 The World Bank. (2018). *Urban population (% of total population) - Australia*. https://data.worldbank.org/indicator/SP.URB.TOTL.IN.ZS?locations=AU

58 Australian Bureau of Statistics. (2018, 12 July). *Census of population and housing: Reflecting Australia - Stories from the census* (Cat. no. 2071.0). https://www.abs.gov.au/ausstats/abs@.nsf/Lookup/2071.0main+features1132016

59 Wolf, K. (2004). Public value of nature: Economics of urban trees, parks and open space. In D. Miller & J. A. Wise. (eds.), *Design with spirit: Proceedings of the 35th annual conference of the Environmental Design Research Association* (pp. 88–92). Environmental Design Research Association.

60 Endreny, T. (2018). Strategically growing the urban forest will improve our world. *Nature Communications*, *9*, 1160. https://doi.org/10.1038/s41467-018-03622-0

61 Feder, S. (2019). *Five important facts about urban forests*. MedForest. https://medforest.net/2019/08/14/five-important-facts-about-urban-forests/

62 Ibid

63 WeConservePA. (n.d.). *Economic benefits of parks*. https://conservationtools.org/guides/98-economic-benefits-of-parks

64 Comer, J. M. (2015). *Garden city*. Zondervan.

65 New South Wales Department of Planning, Industry and Environment. (2018, 17 June). *Parrots*. https://www.environment.nsw.gov.au/topics/animals-and-plants/native-animals/native-animal-facts/parrots

66 Max Planck Society. (2021, 22 July). *Clever cockatoos learn through social interaction*. Phys.org. https://phys.org/news/2021-07-clever-cockatoos-social-interaction.html

67 Birdlife Australia. (n.d.). https://birdlife.org.au/

68 Birdlife Australia. (n.d.). *Creating places for birds*. https://www.birdsinbackyards.net/places

69 Birds in Backyards. (n.d.). *To feed or not to feed*. https://www.birdsinbackyards.net/feed-or-not-feed-0

70 Wildlife Preservation Society of Queensland. (2020, 10 June). *Feeding wild birds in Australia*. https://wildlife.org.au/feeding-wildlife/

71 Gus Speth (chairman of the Council on Environmental Quality under former US president Jimmy Carter), as cited in Richter, S. L. (2020). *Stewards of Eden: What scripture says about the environment and why it matters*. InterVarsity Press.

72 Unify. (2021). '*My people are not threatened by silence. They are completely at home in it. They have lived for thousands of* [Image attached] [Text from M.-R. Ungunmerr Baumann]. Facebook. https://m.facebook.com/unify/photos/a.517823741562555/4911019655576253/

73 Berry, R. J. & Meitzner Yoder, L. S. (2021). *John Stott on creation care*. IVP Books.

74 The Jungle Diaries. (2018, 15 July). *Butterflies drinking turtle tears!?* YouTube. https://www.youtube.com/watch?v=4Dj78JCKlPU

75 Lester, I. (2014, 2 May). *Crocodile tears please butterflies and bees*. Ecological Society of America. https://www.esa.org/esablog/2014/05/02/crocodile-tears-please-butterflies-and-bees/

76 Ibid

77 Ibid

78 Garrett, R., Carlson, K., Goggans, M. S., Nesson, M. H., Shepard, C. A. & Schofield, R. M. S. (2016). Leaf processing behaviour in *Atta* leafcutter ants: 90% of leaf cutting takes place inside the nest, and ants select pieces that require less cutting. *Royal Society Open Science*, *3*(1), Article 150111. https://doi.org/10.1098/rsos.150111

79 Roetzel, L. J. (2021, 5 October). *The caste system and gardening proficiency of leafcutter ants*. One Earth. https://www.oneearth.org/the-caste-system-and-gardening-proficiency-of-leafcutter-ants/

80 McVean, A. (2019, 2 May). *Leafcutter Ants are Farmers Who Grow Fungi*. McGill Office for Science and Society. https://www.mcgill.ca/oss/article/did-you-know/did-you-know-leafcutter-ants-are-farmers-who-grow-fungi

81 Roetzel, L. J. (2021, 5 October). *The caste system and gardening proficiency of leafcutter ants*. One Earth. https://www.oneearth.org/the-caste-system-and-gardening-proficiency-of-leafcutter-ants/

82 McVean, A. (2019, 2 May). *Leafcutter Ants are Farmers Who Grow Fungi*. McGill Office for Science and Society. https://www.mcgill.ca/oss/article/did-you-know/did-you-know-leafcutter-ants-are-farmers-who-grow-fungi

83 Saint Louis Zoo. (n.d.). *Leaf cutter ants*. https://www.stlzoo.org/animals/abouttheanimals/invertebrates/insects/antsbeeswasps/leafcutterant

84 Roetzel, L. J. (2021, 5 October). *The caste system and gardening proficiency of leafcutter ants*. One Earth. https://www.oneearth.org/the-caste-system-and-gardening-proficiency-of-leafcutter-ants/

85 Kimberley Land Council. (n.d.). *Indigenous fire management*. https://www.klc.org.au/indigenous-fire-management

86 Boyd, T. (n.d.). *Birds of fire*. PennState Altoona. https://altoona.psu.edu/feature/birds-fire

87 Bonta, M., Gosford, R., Eussen, D., Ferguson, N., Loveless, E. & Witwer, M. (2017). Intentional fire-spreading by 'firehawk' raptors in Northern Australia. *Journal of Ethnobiology*, *37*(4), 700–718. https://doi.org/10.2993/0278-0771-37.4.700

88 Ibid

89 Hausheer, J. E. (2018, 12 January). *Australian 'firehawk' raptors intentionally spread wildfires.* Cool Green Science. https://blog.nature.org/science/2018/01/12/australian-firehawk-raptors-intentionally-spread-wildfires/

90 Estimated from Urry, L., Meyers, N., Cain, M., Wasserman, S., Minorsky, P. V. & Reece, J. B. (2018). *Campbell biology* (11th ed.). Person Australia.

91 Simard, S., Perry, D., Jones, M., Myrold, D. D., Durall, D. M. & Molina, R. (1997). Net transfer of carbon between tree species with shared ectomycorrhizal fungi. *Nature, 388*, 579–582.

92 Paula, J. R., Otjacques, E., Hildebrandt, C., Grutter, A. S. & Rosa, R. (2020). Ocean acidification does not affect fish ectoparasite survival. *Oceans, 1*, 27–33. https://doi.org/10.3390/oceans1010003

93 Evans, L. (2000). *Labroides dimidiatus: Blue streak.* Animal Diversity Web. https://animaldiversity.org/accounts/Labroides_dimidiatus/

94 What manta rays remember: The best spots to get spruced up. (2021, 8 April). *Nature, 592*, 329. https://doi.org/10.1038/d41586-021-00903-5

95 Cornell University College of Agriculture and Life Sciences. (n.d.). *Insect biology and ecology: A primer.* https://biocontrol.entomology.cornell.edu/bio.php

96 Christian-Albrechts University of Kiel. (2012, 21 February). *Eat and let die: Insect feeds on toxic plants for protection from predators.* ScienceDaily. https://www.sciencedaily.com/releases/2012/02/120221090240.htm

97 Nyffeler, M., Şekercioğlu, Ç. & Whelan, C. (2018). Insectivorous birds consume an estimated 400–500 million tons of prey annually. *The Science of Nature, 105*, Article 47. https://doi.org/10.1007/s00114-018-1571-z

98 Cornell University College of Agriculture and Life Sciences. (n.d.). *Insect biology and ecology: A primer.* https://biocontrol.entomology.cornell.edu/bio.php

99 Snowden, B. (2017, 9 October). *'Planet of insects' must be protected – Prof. Alexey Solodovnikov.* Horizon. https://ec.europa.eu/research-and-innovation/en/horizon-magazine/planet-insects-must-be-protected-prof-alexey-solodovnikov

100 NASA Space Place. (2021, 22 July). *What causes the seasons?* https://spaceplace.nasa.gov/seasons/en/

101 National Oceanic and Atmospheric Administration. (2019, 1 February). *Changing seasons.* https://www.noaa.gov/education/resource-collections/climate/changing-seasons

102 When photographing with a drone in New South Wales national parks, as per their regulations, we always seek prior permission, fly according to the conditions stipulated and comply with all requirements stipulated by the Civil Aviation Safety Authority (https://www.casa.gov.au/drones/drone-rules).

103 New South Wales National Parks & Wildlife Service. (n.d.). *Mount Kaputar National Park.* https://www.nationalparks.nsw.gov.au/visit-a-park/parks/mount-kaputar-national-park/learn-more

104 Ibid

105 Sierra Club. (n.d.). *John Muir: A brief biography.* https://vault.sierraclub.org/john_muir_exhibit/life/muir_biography.aspx

106 Suttie, J. (2016, 2 March). *How nature can make you kinder, happier, and more creative.* Greater Good Magazine. https://greatergood.berkeley.edu/article/item/how_nature_makes_you_kinder_happier_more_creative

107 TEDx Talks. (2017, 13 December). *Restore your brain with nature | David Strayer | TEDxManhattanBeach* [Video]. YouTube. https://www.youtube.com/watch?v=_vRMRBxvtZA

108 TEDx Talks. (2014, 19 April). *Neuroconservation – Your brain on nature: Wallace J. Nichols at TEDxSantaCruz* [Video]. YouTube. https://www.youtube.com/watch?v=r2_X7mTUirk

109 American Foundation for the Blind. (2015, 3 April). *:Nature has the power to renew and refresh..' Helen Keller.* https://www.afb.org/blog/entry/get-out-nature-says-helen-keller

110 First Peoples – State Relations. (2019, 29 September). *William Cooper: A leader of leaders.* https://www.firstpeoplesrelations.vic.gov.au/william-cooper

111 Ambrosio, N. (2016, 7 November). *Helping weary travellers: Migratory birds make some of the world's longest journeys and they face many challenges along the way.* Wing Threads. https://wingthreads.com/helping-weary-travellers/

112 Hohenhaus, R. (2019, 25 March). *Saving Australia's migratory shorebirds from extinction.* The University of Queensland, Australia. http://www.uq.edu.au/research/impact/stories/saving-australias-migratory-shorebirds-from-extinction/

113 Cain, C. (2017, 11 December). *The benefits of dead trees.* Forest Preserve District Will County. https://www.reconnectwithnature.org/news-events/big-features/dead-dying-trees-bring-life-to-the-forest

114 Thorn, S., Seibold, S., Leverkus, A. B., Michler, T., Müller, J., Noss, R. F., Stork, N. Vogel, S. & Lindenmayer, D. B. (2020). The living dead: Acknowledging life after tree death to stop forest degradation. *Frontiers in Ecology and the Environment, 18*(9), 505–512. https://doi.org/10.1002/fee.2252

115 Adam, P. (2019). *Removal of dead wood and dead trees – Key threatening process listing.* New South Wales Department of Planning and Environment. https://www.

environment.nsw.gov.au/topics/animals-and-plants/threatened-species/nsw-threat-ened-species-scientific-committee/determinations/final-determinations/2000-2003/removal-of-dead-wood-and-dead-trees-key-threatening-process-listing

116 Cain, C. (2017, 11 December). *The benefits of dead trees.* Forest Preserve District Will County. https://www.reconnectwithnature.org/news-events/big-features/dead-dying-trees-bring-life-to-the-forest

117 Adam, P. (2019). *Removal of dead wood and dead trees – Key threatening process listing.* New South Wales Department of Planning and Environment. https://www.environment.nsw.gov.au/topics/animals-and-plants/threatened-species/nsw-threat-ened-species-scientific-committee/determinations/final-determinations/2000-2003/removal-of-dead-wood-and-dead-trees-key-threatening-process-listing

118 The Ocean Portal Team. (2020, March). *Whales: Cetacea.* Smithsonian Ocean. https://ocean.si.edu/ocean-life/marine-mammals/whales

119 Marine Education and Research Society. (n.d.). *MERS humpback whale research.* https://www.mersociety.org/humpback

120 International Whaling Commission. (2021). *Humpback whale.* https://wwhand-book.iwc.int/en/species/humpback-whale

121 Neilson, J., Straley, J., Gabriele, C. & Hills, S. (2009). Non-lethal entanglement of humpback whales (*Megaptera novaeangliae*) in fishing gear in northern Southeast Alaska. *Journal of Biogeography*, 36, 452–464. https://doi.org//10.1111/j.1365-2699.2007.01820.x

122 Naessig, P. & Lanyon, J. (2004). Levels and probable origin of predatory scarring on humpback whales (*Megaptera novaeangliae*) in east Australian waters. *Wildlife Research*, 31(2), 163– 170. https://doi.org/10.1071/WR03086

123 Dwyer, S. & Visser, I. (2011). Cookie cutter shark (*Isistius sp.*) bites on cetaceans, with particular reference to killer whales (Orca) (*Orcinus orca*). *Aquatic Mammals*, 37, 111–138. https://doi.org/10.1578/AM.37.2.2011.111

124 Dearnaley, J. (2009). The fungal endophytes of *Erythrorchis cassythoides*—Is this Orchid saprophytic or parasitic? *Australian Mycologist*, 25(2), 51–57.

125 Helmenstine, A. (2021, 5 July). *Commensalism definition and examples.* Sciences Notes and Projects. https://sciencenotes.org/commensalism-definition-and-exam-ples/

126 Department of Regional New South Wales. (2020). *Warrumbungle National Park geotrails.* https://www.regional.nsw.gov.au/meg/community/geotrails/warrumbungle-national-park-geotrails

127 Ibid

128 McTainsh, G. (2011, 18–21 September). *Wind erosion, dust and their environmental impacts: An Australian perspective* [Keynote presentation]. International Symposium on Erosion and Landscape Evolution, Anchorage, Alaska, United States. https://topsoil.nserl.purdue.edu/~flanagan/isele2011/presentations/Keynote-1-McTainsh.pdf

129 Cork, S., Eadie, L., Mele, P., Price, R. & Yule, D. (2012, September). *The relationships between land management practices and soil condition and the quality of ecosystem services delivered from agricultural land in Australia.* Kiri-ganai Research. https://www.agriculture.gov.au/sites/default/files/sitecollectiondocuments/natural-resources/ecosystem-services/chp6_10.pdf

130 Tozer P. & Leys J. (2013). Dust storms – What do they really cost? *The Rangeland Journal*, 35, 131–142. https://doi.org/10.1071/RJ12085

131 Nguyen, H., Riley, M., Leys, J. & Salter, D. (2019). Dust storm event of February 2019 in central and east coast of Australia and evidence of long-range trans-port to New Zealand and Antarctica. *Atmosphere*, 10(11), Article 653. https://doi.org/10.3390/atmos10110653

132 Cork, S., Eadie, L., Mele, P., Price, R. & Yule, D. (2012, September). *The relationships between land management practices and soil condition and the quality of ecosystem services delivered from agricultural land in Australia.* Kiri-ganai Research. https://www.agriculture.gov.au/sites/default/files/sitecollectiondocuments/natural-resources/ecosystem-services/chp6_10.pdf

133 MarineBio. (n.d.). *Day octopuses,* Octopus cyanea. https://www.marinebio.org/species/day-octopuses/octopus-cyanea/

134 Australian Academy of Science. (n.d.). *What is science?* https://www.science.org.au/curious/people-medicine/what-science

135 Bennett, L. (2018, December). *Sea turtles: Cheloniidae and Dermatochelyidae.* Smith-sonian Ocean. https://ocean.si.edu/ocean-life/reptiles/sea-turtles

136 Binns, H. (2016, 9 February). *What's love got to do with it?* The Pew Charitable Trusts. https://www.pewtrusts.org/en/research-and-analysis/articles/2016/02/09/msa-40-whats-love-got-to-do-with-green-sea-turtles-and-fish

137 Bennett, L. (2018, December). *Sea turtles: Cheloniidae and Dermatochelyidae.* Smith-sonian Ocean. https://ocean.si.edu/ocean-life/reptiles/sea-turtles

138 Costello, T. (2021, 22 November). *If Scott Morrison acted on his strong Christian faith, he would phase out coal.* The Guardian. https://www.theguardian.com/commentisfree/2021/nov/22/if-scott-morrison-acted-on-his-strong-christian-faith-he-would-phase-out-coal

139 Department of Biodiversity, Conservation and Attractions. (2020). *Recovery plans and interim recovery plans.* Government of Western Australia. https://www.dpaw.wa.gov.au/plants-and-animals/threatened-species-and-communities/wa-s-threatened-ecological-communities

140 Birdlife Australia. (2020). *Shorebirds identification booklet.*

141 Schiffner I., Perez T. & Srinivasan M. (2016). Strategies for pre-emptive mid-air

collision avoidance in budgerigars. *PLOS ONE, 11*(9), Article e0162435. https://doi.org/10.1371/journal.pone.0162435

142 The Cornell Lab. (2009). *Why don't birds collide when they are flying close together in tight flocks?* Cornell University. https://www.allaboutbirds.org/news/why-dont-birds-collide-when-they-are-flying-close-together-in-tight-flocks/

143 McDonald, P. J., Brittingham, R., Nano, C. & Paltridge, R. (2015). A new population of the critically endangered central rock-rat (*Zyzomys pedunculatus*) discovered in the Northern Territory. *Australian Mammalogy, 37*, 97–100. https://doi.org/10.1071/AM14012

144 Murphy, B. P., Woolley, L.-A., Geyle, H. M., Legge, S. M., Palmer, R., Dickman, C. R., Augusteyn, J., Brown, S. C., Comer, S., Doherty, T. S., Eager, C., Edwards, G., Fordham, D. A., Harley, D., McDonald, P. J., McGregor, H., Moseby, K. E., Myers, C., … Woinzarski, J. C. Z. (2019). Introduced cats (*Felis catus*) eating a continental fauna: The number of mammals killed in Australia. *Biological Conservation, 237*, 28–40. https://doi.org/10.1016/j.biocon.2019.06.013

145 Department of Environment and Natural Resources, Northern Territory. (2018). *National recovery plan for the central rock-rat* Zyzomys pedunculatus. Australian Government Department of Agriculture, Water and the Environment. https://www.awe.gov.au/environment/biodiversity/threatened/publications/recovery/central-rock-rat-2018

146 Australian Government Department of Agriculture, Water and the Environment. (n.d.). *History of whaling in Australia.* https://www.environment.gov.au/marine/marine-species/cetaceans/whaling

147 Australian Government Department of Agriculture, Water and the Environment. (2009). *The eastern humpback whales of eastern Australia.* https://www.environment.gov.au/marine/publications/humpback-whales-eastern-australia

148 Australian Government Department of Agriculture, Water and the Environment. (2021). *Consultation document on eligibility for delisting* Megaptera novaeangliae *(humpback whale).* https://www.awe.gov.au/environment/biodiversity/threatened/nominations/comment/megaptera-novaeangliae

149 Barth, as cited in Moo, D. J. & Moo, J. A. (2018). *Creation care: A biblical theology of the natural world.* Zondervan.

150 Díaz, S., Settele, J., Brondízio, E., Ngo, H. T., Guèze, M., Agard, J., Arneth, A., Balvanera, P., Brauman, K., Butchart, S., Chan, K., Garibaldi, L. A., Ichii, K., Liu, J., Subramanian, S. M., Midgley, G. F., Miloslavich, P., Molnár, Z., Obura, D., … Zayas, C. (2019). *The global assessment report on biodiversity and ecosystem services. Summary for policymakers.* Intergovernmental Science-Policy Platform on Biodiversity and Ecosystem Services. https://ipbes.net/sites/default/files/inline/files/ipbes_global_assessment_report_summary_for_policymakers.pdf. *Note*: This report was compiled by 145 expert authors from 50 countries over 3 years. It was also based on a systematic review of about 15,000 scientific and government sources

151 Food and Agriculture Organization of the United Nations and United Nations Environment Programme. (2020). *The state of the world's forests 2020: Forests, biodiversity and people.* https://doi.org/10.4060/ca8642en

152 United Nations Sustainable Development Goals. (2019, 6 May). *UN report: Nature's dangerous decline 'unprecedented'; species extinction rates 'accelerating'* https://www.un.org/sustainabledevelopment/blog/2019/05/nature-decline-unprecedented-report/

153 Food and Agriculture Organization of the United Nations and United Nations Environment Programme. (2020). *The state of the world's forests 2020: Forests, biodiversity and people.* https://doi.org/10.4060/ca8642en

154 United Nations Sustainable Development Goals. (2019, 6 May). *UN report: Nature's dangerous decline 'unprecedented'; species extinction rates 'accelerating'* https://www.un.org/sustainabledevelopment/blog/2019/05/nature-decline-unprecedented-report/

155 Ibid

156 Valerio, R. (January 12, 2020). *Pig ignorant to egghead: How I learnt to live more simply.* https://ruthvalerio.net/green-living-2/pig-ignorant-to-egg-head-how-a-christian-can-live-more-simply/

Photo: Descending from Mueller Hut, Aoraki/Mt Cook National Park, New Zealand

'What is needed is a posture of attentiveness and wonder to the world around us that honours God and his creation, that recalls us to our true identity, and that can, if we let it, open up vistas of joy and possibility in our lives.'

(Moo, D.J. and Moo, J.A. *Creation Care (Biblical Theology for Life)* (p. 224). Zondervan Academic. Kindle Edition.

Ingram Content Group UK Ltd.
Milton Keynes UK
UKRC031102270323
419229UK00001B/1